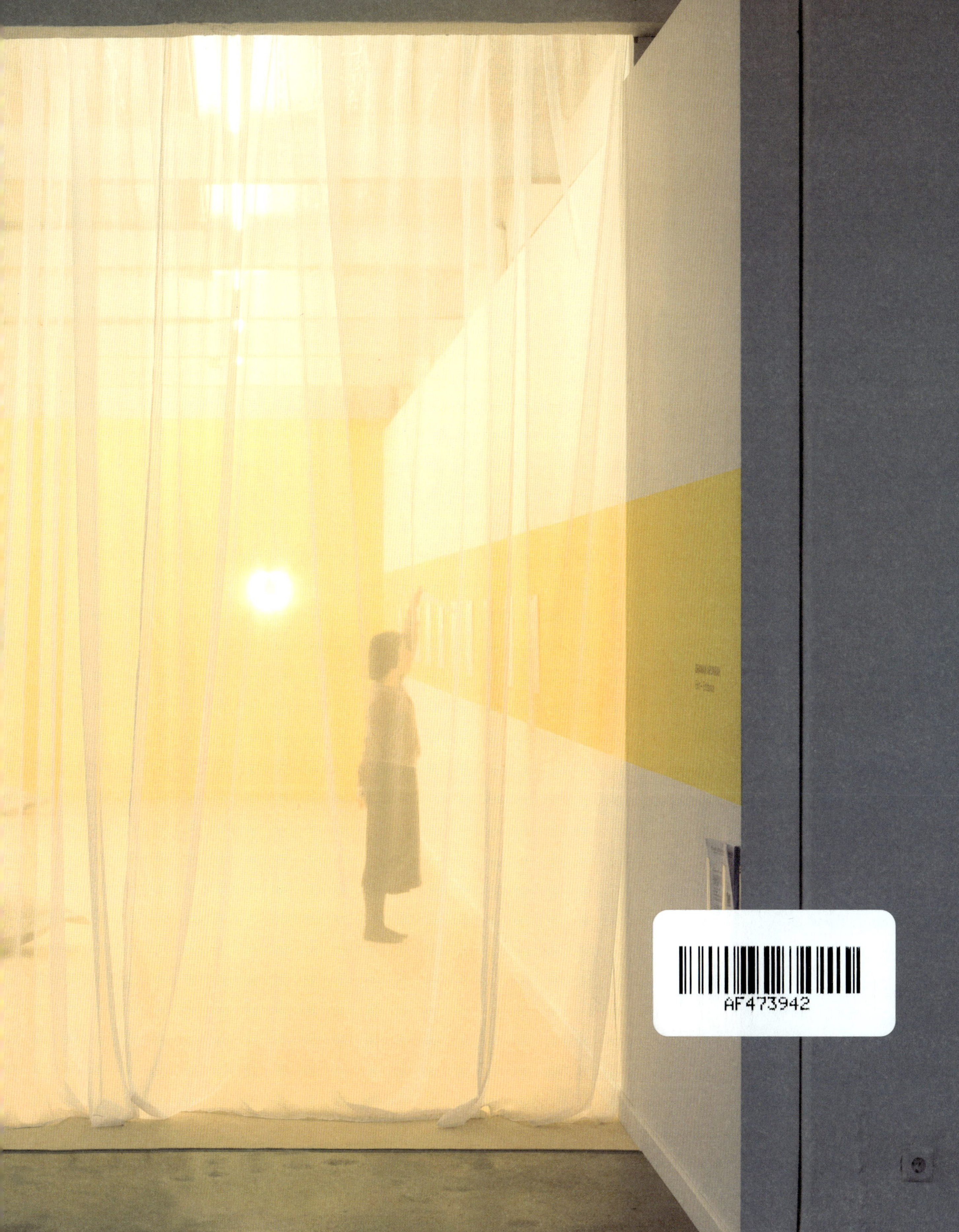

A House is Inside Me: Meandering and Slowness in the Work of Orawan Arunrak

Roger Nelson

There is one small detail in Orawan Arunrak's latest solo exhibition, *Exit – Entrance*, which may be considered a synecdoche of the recurring concerns of her practice over the past decade. It is a QR code, which when scanned directs viewers to an online translation of the four different languages that are used in the sound installation, *Exit – Entrance* (2017), which envelops the exhibition. "In the exhibition, it's okay if you can understand, and it's okay if you get lost," the artist explains. The voices, speaking English, German, Thai and Vietnamese, are interwoven to form what Orawan describes as a "conversation collage," in which sentences merge together.[1]

That it is a QR code that I am proposing as an emblematic entry point to Orawan's practice may be surprising to those who know the artist's work, which has been exhibited in eight countries to date, including in many of the most respected galleries and museums in her native Thailand. After all, pen and paper are Orawan's constant companions, and her work has generally eschewed all but the most simple and familiar of technologies. She prides herself on having often created conceptually and processually complex projects on a zero budget, and feels this sets her apart from many other artists of her generation, in Thailand as elsewhere, who are often drawn to more elaborate and costly materials and scale. How then, can this QR code be understood as indicative of Orawan's practice? There are three ways.

The first is simple: in requiring visitors to scan it in order to access the information that it initially conceals yet later reveals, a QR code encourages an active response from the exhibition visitor. Whether it is asking viewers to bend down low to see a drawing hung close to the floor, as in *What Are They Doing Inside?* (2013), or obscuring images within bottles and wooden drawers and notebooks, as in *Breathing Bubbles* (2013), *Follow Me* (2013), and *Come In* (2014), Orawan consistently presents her work in a manner which demands an active bodily engagement from her viewers. She has also on numerous occasions included elements which—like the QR code—direct her audiences to engage further the work at a later moment, while outside of the exhibition space. Both *What Are They Doing Inside?* and an earlier project called *Drifting Map of Bangkok* (2012), for example, included specific street addresses, which Orawan asked her viewers to visit in order to appreciate the locally-specific references in her drawings.

1 Unless otherwise indicated, all quotes from Orawan Arunrak are from interviews and email correspondence conducted during February, March and April 2017. This text also draws on numerous conversations held since April 2014, in Bangkok, Phnom Penh, Ho Chi Minh City, Singapore, and elsewhere. I warmly thank the artist for her tireless generosity in answering my questions so patiently, eloquently and insightfully. Thanks also to Nicola Müllerschön, Thorsten Probst, Brian Curtin, Gridthiya Gaweewong, and Arin Rungjang.

A second aspect of the QR code which typifies the artist's practice is the fact that the translation to which it directs visitors will only be made available a week after the exhibition opens. This demands from the visitor a good deal of patience, a slow pondering, a return to the ideas and content of the exhibition, if not to the exhibition space itself. This desire to slow down the experience of the artwork is at the heart of Orawan's practice, as we shall see.

The final way in which the QR code illuminates Orawan's work more broadly is in its cosmopolitanism, which draws from the artist's itinerant practice.[2] The QR code, after all, links to the translation of words spoken by ten different people in Orawan's *Exit - Entrance* sound installation. These ten people who hail from multiple locations, speak many different languages, and embody diverse and plural cultures. English, German, Thai and Vietnamese are all spoken in *Exit - Entrance*, and no translation is provided to the gallery-goer other than the one made belatedly available by scanning the QR code. For many visitors, therefore, the words being spoken upon entry into the exhibition space will be initially unintelligible, and only those patient enough to wait for the speaker—and thus the language—to change will have a chance to listen to words in a language they can understand. The work may be understood as a celebration of the aesthetic qualities of the different languages, or of the pleasure that can be derived from listening to that which we do not understand: of not knowing, or of the impossibility of knowing.

Taking its cue from the meandering and slow nature of Orawan's practice, this essay will examine these cornerstones of the artist's work in a deliberately roundabout manner. In focusing on these elements, I am necessarily

2 My understanding of cosmopolitanism is informed by my former doctoral co-supervisor at the University of Melbourne, Nikos Papastergiadis. See: Nikos Papastergiadis, *Cosmopolitanism and Culture* (Cambridge, UK and Malden, MA: 2012). See also: Nikos Papastergiadis, *The Turbulence of Migration* (Cambridge, UK and Malden, MA: Polity Press, 2000).

What Are They Doing Inside?, 2013

setting aside many other facets of her work. These include: her consistent engagement with sites and rituals associated with Southeast Asian practices of Buddhism, her interest in the gendered nature of bodily experience and its representation, and the shift in her drawing style from a more straightforwardly observational and representational mode, pursued until 2016, to an exploration of more abstracted and open-ended forms, in her most recent projects. These are all rich sites for further inquiry. I choose to concentrate instead on Orawan's peripatetic process and cosmopolitan approach, and her engagement with and slowing down of the viewing experience, as I take these elements to be especially resonant with the practices of other artists of her generation, working within and beyond the multiple settings in which she circulates.

We will turn now to look in more detail at *Breathing Bubbles*, another work I take to be emblematic of the meandering and slowness in Orawan's work, before considering some other projects, investigating the notion of the "house" and "home" in the artist's practice, and finally returning to *Exit - Entrance*.

At first glance, there seemed to be nothing much to see. For those visiting a festival-style event called *The Performing Arts Meeting* in Yokohama's Kanagawa Arts Theatre in 2013, to begin with all that appeared of Orawan Arunrak's *Breathing Bubbles* (2013) was a haphazard assortment of empty glass bottles, placed along an unadorned raw concrete ledge.

Upon closer inspection, however, it became apparent that the bottles were not, in fact, empty. Inside each one was a tiny drawing—and sometimes several—rendered in simple black and white on torn scraps of paper. Curled into the bottles, the drawings were not always easily identifiable, but they included sketches of objects, crea-

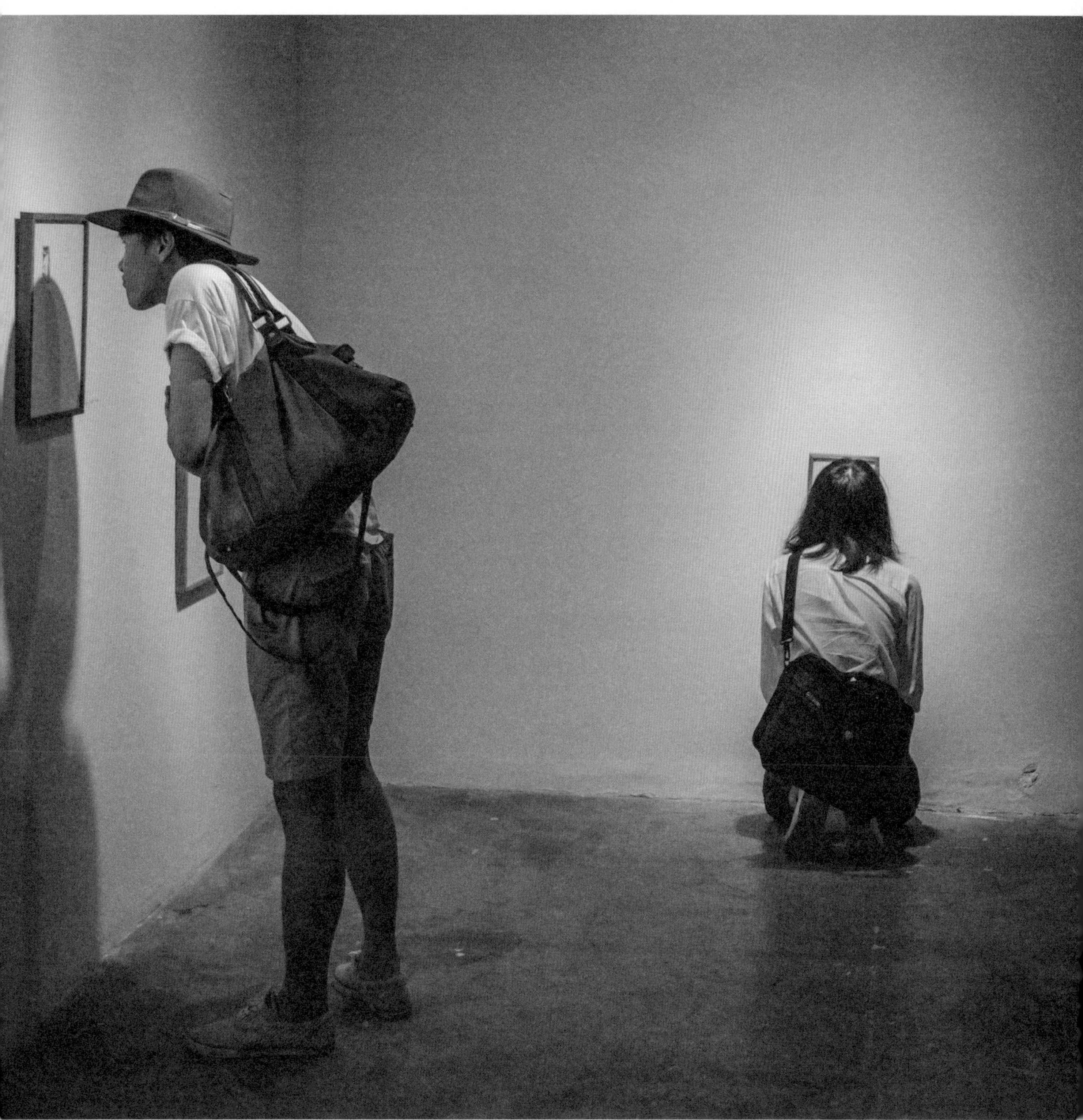

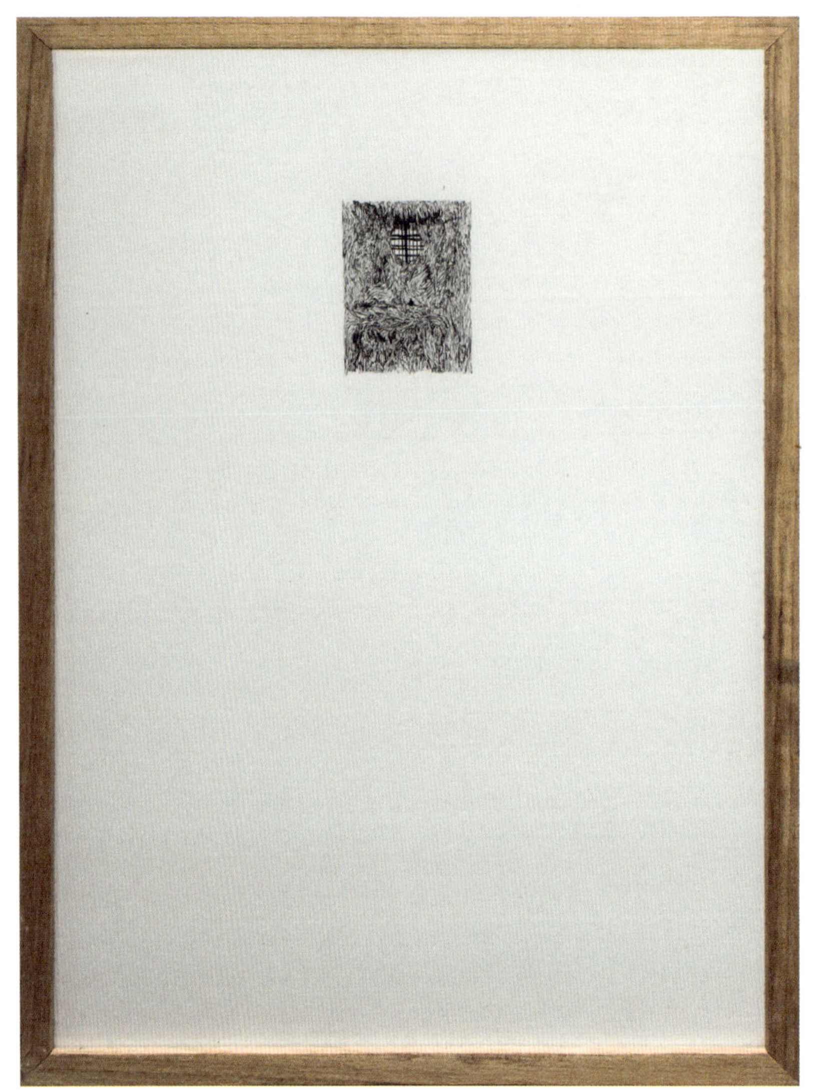

What Are They Doing Inside?, 2013

tures, and other detritus, as well as some doodles less easy to identify. This was a seemingly arbitrary "feed" of images, appearing as if culled from various online and urban environments. Orawan describes the images as "random," and suggests that as a result, viewers were prompted to "imagine the story by themselves." She continues that, for her, "this [was] a good platform to see people sharing and creating stories and situations together."

In order to see these drawings—which were captivating in their unexpectedness, even if the images themselves were somewhat inscrutable, even unexceptional—visitors were forced to pick up one of the bottles. Each bottle was different, and needed to be held aloft at a different angle to bring the drawing inside into view. Since the bottles were glass, and arranged along a ledge of concrete, some care needed to be taken; but since they were arranged in a fairly tight formation, interaction not only with the objects but with fellow visitors was inevitable. A small queue formed, since this process took some time, and with it came friendly jostling and the exchanges of glances and comments among the visitors, both friends and strangers alike. Crucially, *Breathing Bubbles* could not be grasped through a quick or passing glance; instead, visitors needed to slow down, and gradually take in the elements of the work.

It was this call for an active yet slowed down engagement and interaction—with the artwork itself, but also between its viewers, and between the artist and her "temporary home"—that was at the heart of *Breathing Bubbles*, and is at the heart of Orawan's practice.[3] "Every work of mine [is] always going in this way," the artist explains. "I need to create my work so that people have to stay and spend time."

3 Orawan speaks often of her many "temporary homes," in reference to the ease with which she shifts between locations. The phrase recalls artist Robert Montgomery's (born 1972) project for the 2011 Venice Biennale, *All Palaces are Temporary Palaces*. Later reproduced on K-pop t-shirts, this poetic phrase was also taken up by another Bangkok-based artist and friend of Orawan's, Henry Tan, in a photo album which circulated widely on social media.

It is not only the viewers of Orawan's work that are asked to "spend time": she too unfailing devotes a great deal of time to personal interactions in the making of her work. Along with installation images of *Breathing Bubbles*, she likes to show photographs she took of the men who collect glass bottles for recycling in Yokohama. Her curiosity about their lives in this unfamiliar city, and her conversations with them, were fundamental to the conceptualization of the piece.

This approach recurs in almost all of her projects from recent years. To make *Come In* (2014), for example, Orawan visited dozens of apartments neighbouring her "temporary home" in the iconic Phnom Penh apartment complex known as the White Building. The artist's drawings of the often cramped yet elaborately decorated interiors of these neighbouring apartments were displayed as part of an installation of furniture borrowed from the neighbours themselves, and fruits bought at the market within the community. The names and addresses of those engaged in the project accompanied many of the drawings in the installation, written in their own handwriting, in both English and Khmer.

Let us return to *Breathing Bubbles*. In addition to embodying the emphasis on slow participation that is central to Orawan's practice, this project for The Performing Arts Meeting was also her first time to work outside of Thailand. Thus, *Breathing Bubbles* marks the beginning of a prolonged and ongoing period of international itinerancy for the artist. Shortly after this visit to Yokohama, Orawan returned to Japan for a solo exhibition in Tokyo, titled *Dear Duang Daao* (2014).

She then embarked on a series of residencies that she playfully conceived as "following in the footsteps of the Buddha." Beginning in Sri Lanka, she continued to Cambodia, spending two months in residency at Phnom Penh's Sa Sa Art Projects. From there, she travelled to Vietnam, for a six-month residency at Ho Chi Minh

City's Sàn Art.[4] She spent time in Chiang Mai, a city in Thailand's north known for its high concentration of artists and art spaces, and also in the Laotian capital of Vientiane. In each of these places, Orawan rapidly attached herself to a diverse range of communities, finding a new "temporary home." Long after the formal residency period ended, she returned again and again to visit her friends and adoptive "family" in each of these Southeast Asian cities. In 2015, Orawan enlisted as a Buddhist nun in a temple outside of Bangkok. Her project there was to work on four interrelated series of works, titled *Meditating Painting; Cleaning, Praying; Keeping, Waiting, Hiding; and Growing, Changing* (all works 2014-2016), which were shown together in the solo exhibition *Zones and Verbs* at Cartel, in Bangkok.

The prevalence of present-tense verbs in these titles—and indeed in the titles for many of Orawan's projects—is indicative of her interest in process, and her attempt to foreground both her working process, and the viewing process, in the exhibition of her work. The abstract circular form of *Meditating Painting*, for example, takes on connotations of cyclical movement—in both Buddhist philosophical terms, and in bodily migration—when exhibited alongside photographs and video footage of different environments in flux, captured in six different Southeast Asian and Asian nations. Its restricted, greyscale palette and display on the easel on which it was painted both imply that the canvas may be still unfinished, or is perhaps unfinishable, while also playfully gesturing to the anachronistic nature of the format of an easel painting on canvas in this era of digital imagery and conceptual artistic practices.

4 Established in 2010, Sa Sa Art Projects is Phnom Penh's only artist-run space. Its co-founders are Khvay Samnang, a former KfW Stiftung grantee and 2014-15 artist-in-residence at Künstlerhaus Bethanien, as well as Lim Sokchanlina, and Vuth Lyno, who serves as Artistic Director. Their residency program, which is primarily focused on Cambodian and Southeast Asian artists, is called "Pisaot" and emphasizes experimentation and community engagement. See: www.sasaart.info.
Sàn Art was established in Ho Chi Minh City in 2007, by artists Dinh Q Le, Tuan Andrew Nguyen, Phunam and Tiffany Chung. Their residency program, called "Sàn Art Laboratory," operated from 2012 to 2015, was focused on Vietnamese and Southeast Asian artists, and directed by curator Zoe Butt. See: www.san-art.org/about-2.

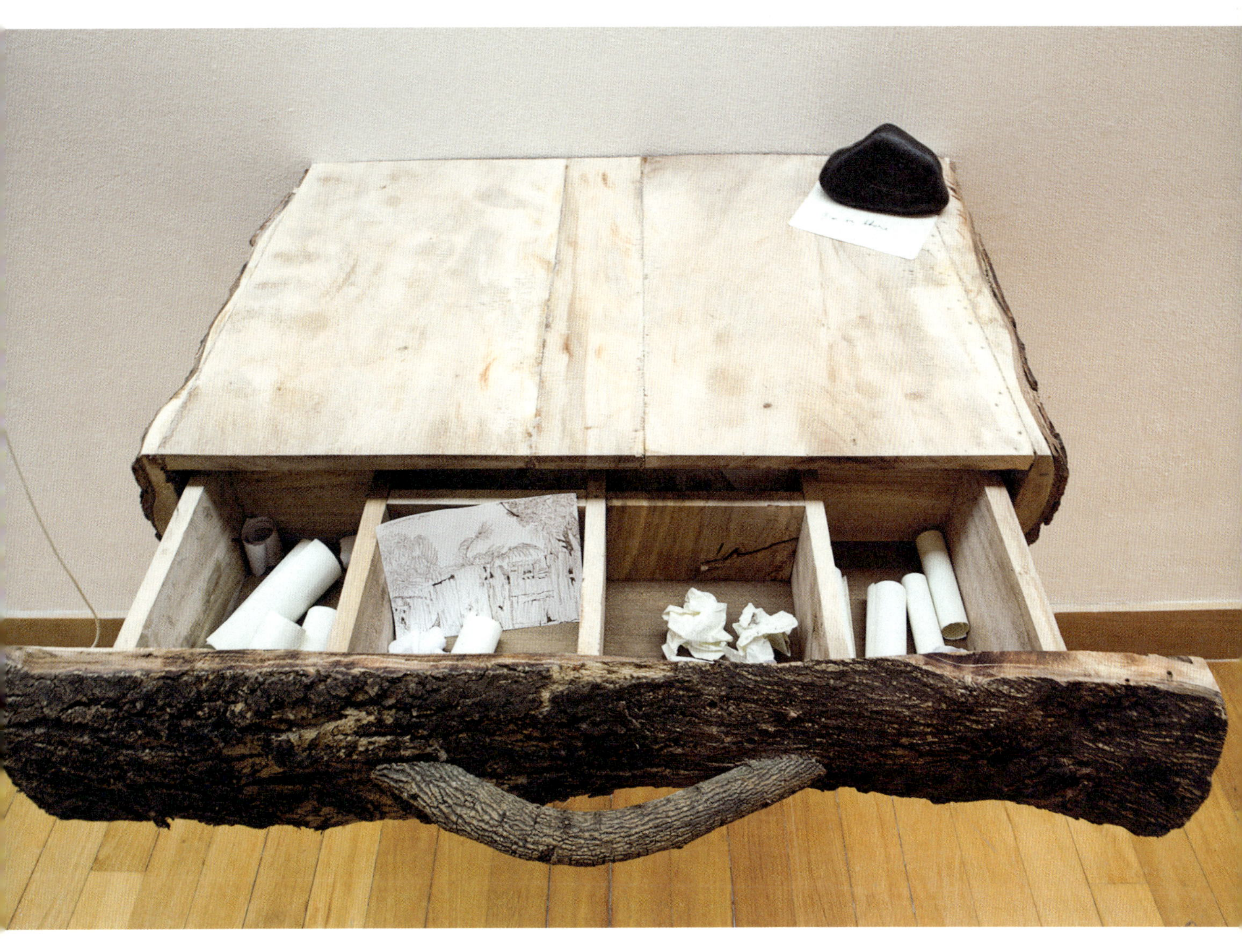

Follow Me, 2013

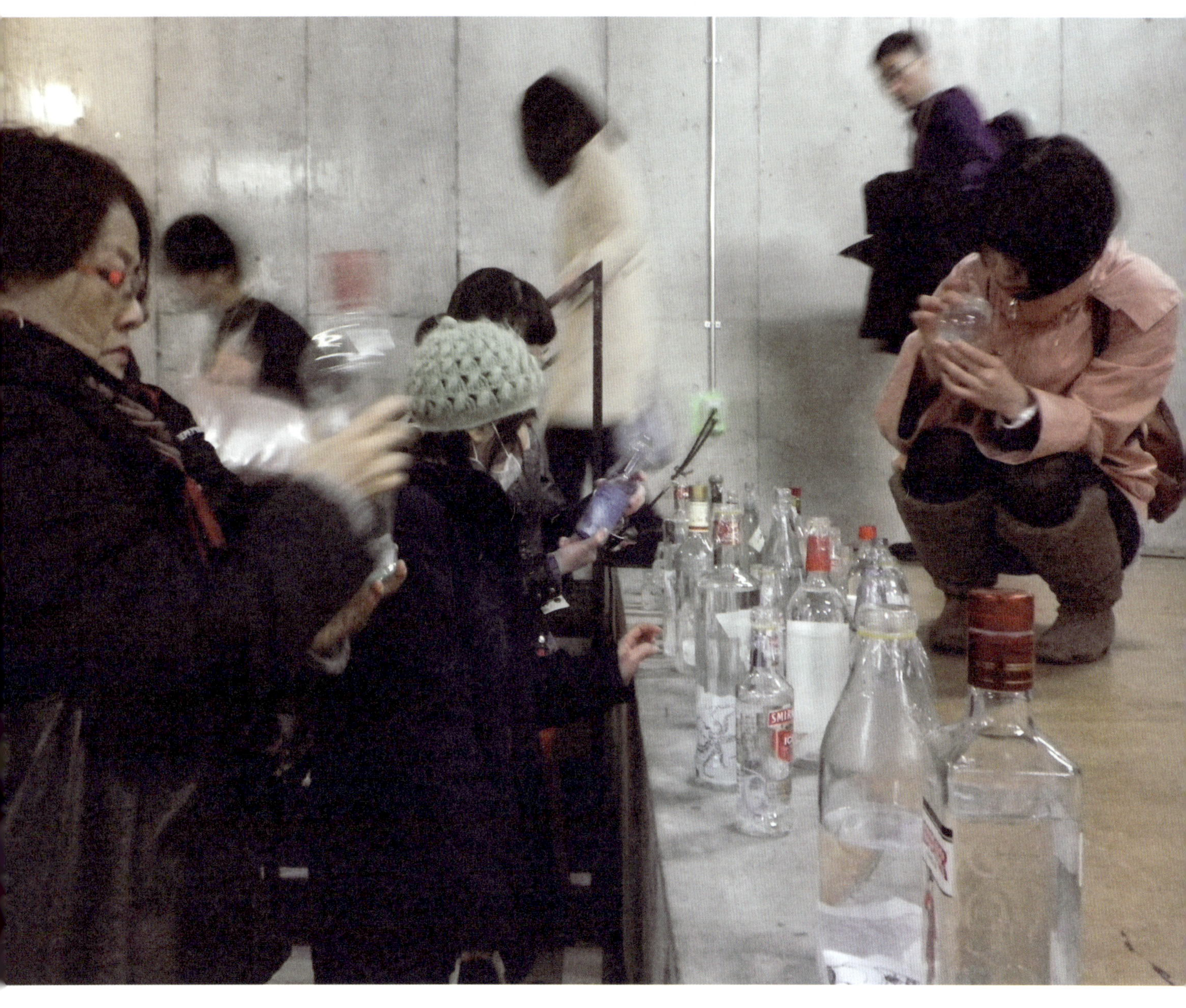

Breathing Bubbles, 2013

For Orawan, as for many other artists of her generation, movement has become an essential condition for creative practice.[5] Her own migration between diverse locations mirrors the networked nature of contemporary cultural life, in which artists are increasingly expected to travel to exhibitions in diverse locations, as well as to undertake international residencies. Orawan's perpetual meandering also points to various other forms of transience, transnational connection, and exchange which she engages with in her work.

While an increased mobility in the world of contemporary art is a seemingly global phenomenon, the itinerancy of contemporary artists from Southeast Asia is additionally compounded by a widespread sense that official arts education in the region benefits from the augmentation offered by the learning opportunities that residencies offer. "Travelling time, residency time is a big classroom for me," Orawan explains. She rarely speaks of her studies in the Department Of Fine Arts at King Mongkut's Institute of Technology, Ladkrabang. Only in preparing for *Exit – Entrance* did Orawan reflect that she was glad of her decision to major in printmaking. "Printmaking is a kind of planning: layers, time, proofs, waiting... be patient," she explains. In preparing the wallpaper for her installation at Künstlerhaus Bethanien, she found her thoughts returning to her studies, and even consulted with one of her former teachers there. "I'm still learning with many things," she happily admits.

Alongside her formal studies, and continuing through her years of international residencies, Orawan has embarked on a dedicated program of self-study, reading numerous philosophers and critical theorists from a range of scholarly traditions. Chief among them, in terms of their impact on her—and their prominence in discussions among Thai intellectuals more broadly—are Gaston Bachelard, Benedict Anderson, and the widely-cited Bangkok-born, US-based scholar Thongchai Winichakul.[6]

Orawan's embrace of itinerancy as not only a necessary condition for practice but also a conceptual premise in her artwork—insofar as it may be understood as a reflection on the increased mobility that characterizes the contemporary—necessitates a revisiting of Bachelard's influential monograph, *The Poetics of Space*. Bachelard famously set out to "show that the house is one of the greatest powers of integration for the thoughts, memories and dreams of [hu]mankind."[7] He proposed that "thanks to the house, a great many of our memories are housed, and if the house is a bit elaborate, if it has a cellar and a garret, nooks and corridors, our memories have refuges that are all the more clearly delineated."[8] The architectural details that Bachelard lists here reveal the European and inevitably Eurocentric frame of reference from which he was writing. As Kuan-Hsing Chen reminds us, European philosophers "have been doing studies in relation to their own living spaces," or, in effect, "doing European studies," since "European experiences were their system of reference." Chen calls on readers to "recognize how extremely limited the current conditions of knowledge are," and insists that "theory too much be deimperialized."[9]

Not only must Bachelard's claims for the intertwining of (unspokenly, but unmistakably, European) experiences and memories and (European) houses be "deimperialized" and rethought for Asian and diverse other con-

5 I have explored these ideas further in a recent project I curated for Bangkok's Jim Thompson Art Center, comprising an exhibition, bilingual lecture series, and a bilingual catalogue published by the James H.W. Thompson Foundation. Titled *People, Money, Ghosts (Movement as Metaphor)*, the exhibition featured artists Khvay Samnang, Amy Lien & Enzo Camacho, and Nguyen Thi Thanh Mai, and ran from 7 March to 18 June 2017.

6 Benedict Anderson, *Imagined Communities: Reflections on the Origin and Spread of Nationalism*, revised edition (London and New York: Verso, 2006 [1983]). Gaston Bachelard, *The Poetics of Space*, translated by Maria Jolas (Boston: Beacon Press, 1994 [1958]). Thongchai Winichakul, *Siam Mapped: A History of the Geo-Body of a Nation* (Honolulu: University of Hawaii Press, 1994).

7 Bachelard, *Poetics*, 6.

8 Bachelard, *Poetics*, 8.

9 Kuan-Hsing Chen, *Asia as Method: Toward Deimperialization* (Durham and London: Duke University Press, 2010), 3.

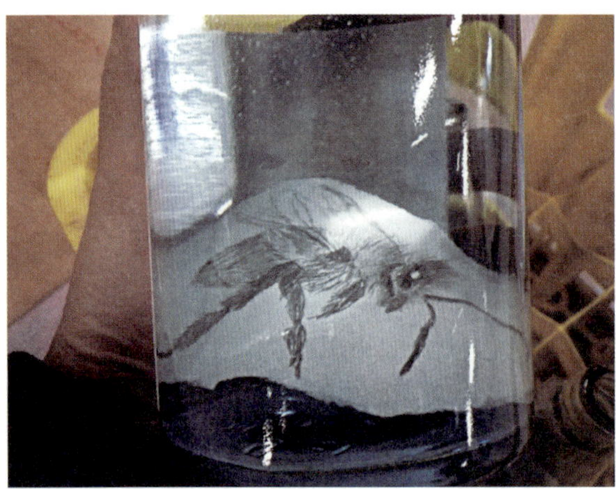

Breathing Bubbles, 2013

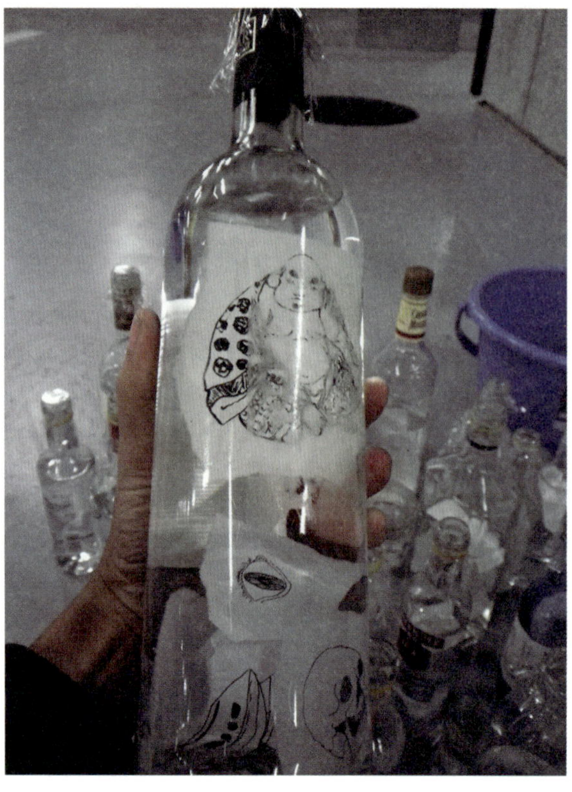

texts, but also—and this is just as crucial—his thinking about the nature of the house must be tested against the shifted conditions of housing that predominate in the twenty-first century globalized neoliberal contemporary. In Europe or elsewhere, after all, does anyone but the smallest elite now live in a house with "a cellar and a garret"? As rates of single occupancy and mixed-use housing increase in many cities globally, how are our memories—often memories inhering in multiple sites—to be "housed"?

Orawan's practice offers one way into these complex and challenging questions. She has a recurrent interest in home environments, most apparent in *Come In* and *What Are They Doing Inside?*, as discussed above, but also informing the overall plan of her *Exit – Entrance* installation, which transforms the white cube gallery into a more intimate space, reminiscent of a domestic setting. Yet despite this interest in the spaces in which people live, Orawan herself has been without a fixed address for several years, living instead in a series of "temporary homes." Her comments on the idea of the house offer a fascinating counterpoint to (or, perhaps, updating of) Bachelard's. "A house is not one place," she affirms. "It's not just a roof over my head. A house is inside me. It can be any place."

It is not only houses and domestic spaces that fascinate Orawan; her work is also deeply informed by her observations of the environments in which art is exhibited, and the behaviours of visitors to galleries and museums. We have seen that her works consistently call on an active interaction from viewers, and consistently seek to "slow down" the experience of engaging with the work. Orawan suggests that this is likely influenced from her years working at the Bangkok Art and Culture Center (BACC), a *kunsthalle*-esque space which is one of the preeminent exhibition venues in the Thai capital. Soon after graduating in 2008, Orawan began to work in the newly opened BACC as an exhibition guide. The space, which (like the National Visual Arts Gallery in Kuala Lumpur) is designed around a spiral ramp that invites inevitable comparisons with the Solomon R. Guggenheim Museum in New York, was at the time "very new for people," Orawan recalls, and "contemporary art still

[felt] very fresh for audiences in Thailand." She quickly progressed from exhibition guide to a coordinating role, and was Assistant Curator from 2011 until 2013.

During her five years of working at the BACC (and also occasionally in other art spaces), Orawan focused on observing the behaviours of exhibition visitors. She repeatedly noticed that people "walk so fast and don't really focus on the artwork." She relates this phenomenon to the general escalation of contemporary life: "our world has started to be very quick, and many people can concentrate for only a short time." Orawan's response was to "want to do something to make audiences stop and take time for a bit, also they can find out the way to see in a very natural way. I need to create the moment to help people stay and focus on something," and also to look outside of the ubiquitous portable screens of contemporary life.

We see this impulse to slow down in all of Orawan's projects, including in her latest and most ambitious, *Exit – Entrance*. This deliberative engagement with the process of experiencing art is not unrelated to the other cornerstone I am proposing for her practice, namely, its translocally roving nature. For Orawan approaches her practice as a way not only to engage with her audiences, but also for herself to "stop and take time for a bit," and "see in a very natural way."

The ten individuals whose voices we hear in *Exit – Entrance* agreed to participate in Orawan's project only after a prolonged period of interaction. Most of it was not focused on her status as an artist seeking participants, but rather was a simple and natural process of building trust by forming friendship. These ten individuals were not chosen by Orawan, she insists, but rather they chose her—this is how she views the chance manner in which she came to connect with each of them. Several of them lead lives that overlap in other ways, as well. Orawan suggests we relate the ten different voices and their stories to the ten different forms that appear on

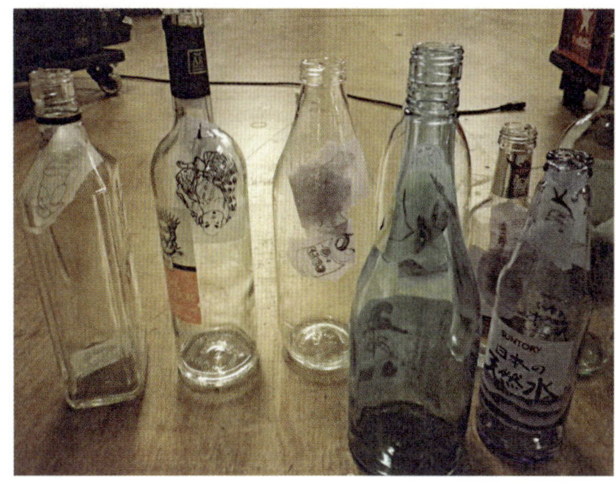

the wallpaper in the installation. These forms are organic and semi-abstract, suggestive but elusive. The artist conceived each form in relation to each conversation, and she wants us to look at these images on the wallpaper while we listen to the "conversation collage," much of which we may not be able to linguistically understand. Perhaps the sense of unknowing and unknowability we feel while we listen may be echoed while we look. The slippages between comprehension and confusion become seductive, and insist on the intertwining of affective and cerebral responses to the work.

Seductive, too, are the warm hues of the walls, at once earthy and fleshy. How this too may be woven into the "conversation collage" is not immediately clear, and is surely not meant to be. It, too, may take some time.

By way of conclusion to this meandering text about the meandering nature of Orawan's practice—its emphasis on slow engagement, and its basis in itinerant and cosmopolitan movement—I propose simply to introduce these ten individuals. In knowing just the barest details of their lives, we will realise, of course, that we do not know them at all. In hearing their voices in the installation—speaking English, German, Thai, and Vietnamese—we may have a similar feeling.

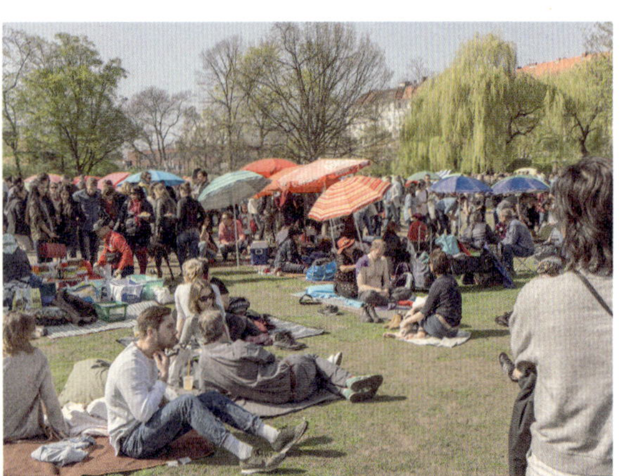

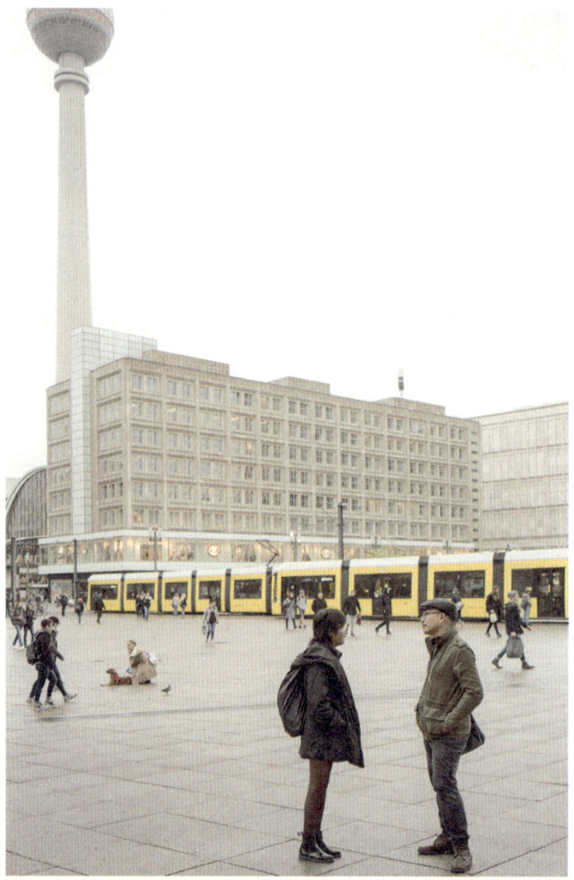

Orawan met a 42-year-old Thai woman, who works in a Thai restaurant, at Berlin's Thai Park on Brandenburgische Strasse. They ate noodles together. The woman told Orawan that she had had two husbands, both Vietnamese: one from the north, and one from the south. This woman speaks with her family in German.

Orawan met a Thai man, 37 years old, through a mutual friend: the internationally acclaimed senior Thai artist, Mit Jai Inn. The man is a doctoral candidate at the Free University of Berlin, and formerly a lecturer in Thailand, including at the Chiang Mai University, in the north of Thailand and near Mit Jai Inn's home and studio. This man brought Orawan to a Thai Buddhist temple, and often helps her with practical advice for life in Berlin. Orawan met a Thai Buddhist monk, 38 years old, on her visit to the Thai temple with the man described above. The monk had previously studied about Buddhism at Chiang Mai University.

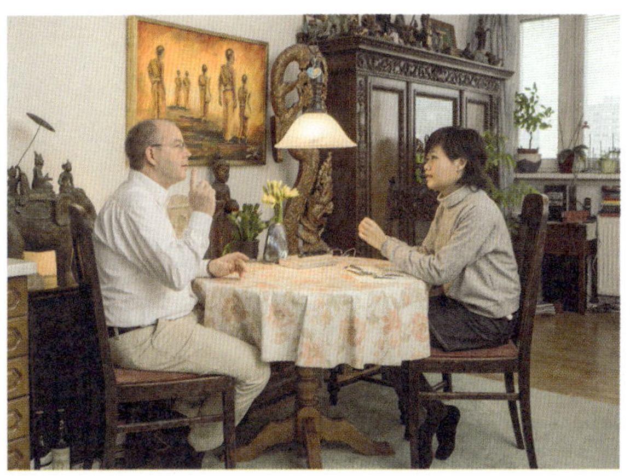

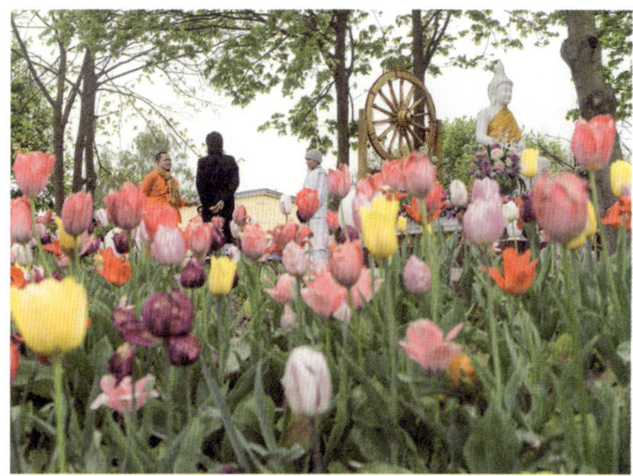

Orawan met a 53-year-old German man when visiting the Thai man in his home; the two are roommates. An anthropologist, the man decorates his living space with objects from Asia. He speaks several languages.

Orawan met a 50-year-old Thai Buddhist nun in the Thai temple. She seemed very open and easy to talk with. This nun is responsible for the cooking and cleaning in the temple, and for shopping for supplies. Her role in the temple is very important.

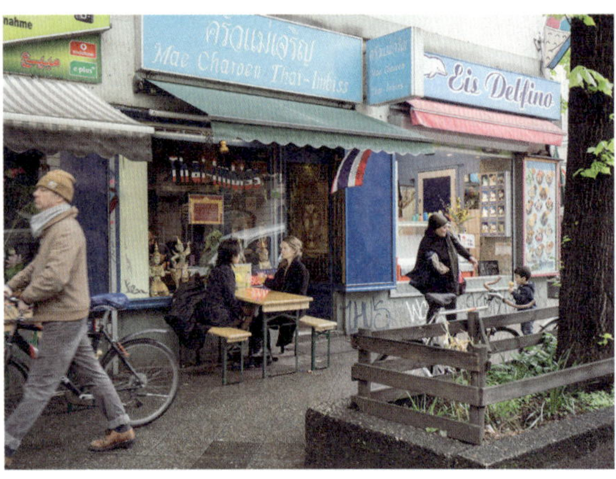

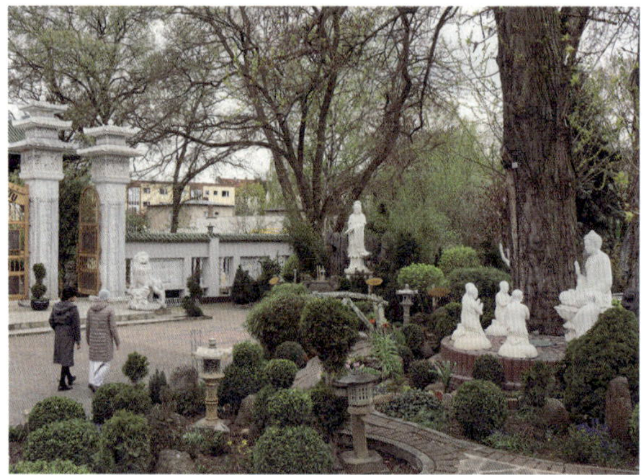

Orawan already knew a 31-year-old German woman before she arrived to Berlin: the two had formerly been roommates in Bangkok.

Orawan met a 41-year-old Vietnamese Buddhist nun after her curiosity about the Vietnamese community in Berlin had been aroused by the Thai woman with the two husbands. Before visiting the temple where the nun lives, Orawan had watched some videos online. The nun had appeared in one of these short documentary films. Orawan met a German Buddhist monk while visiting the Thai temple. She had many questions for him.

Orawan met a 29-year-old Vietnamese woman in 2015, but they never had a chance to talk. They met again in 2016, when the woman visited Poland while Orawan was there to exhibit her work. Having lived in Ho Chi Minh City for six months, Orawan enjoyed the chance to talk with this woman, who had previously worked at a leading art and film centre in Hanoi, called DocLab.

Orawan met another Vietnamese woman, also in 2015, while she was in Ho Chi Minh City. This woman had grown up in Berlin from the age of 13 to 30. A fine art school graduate, she is now living in Ho Chi Minh City, working in fashion. She will return to Germany soon.

The artist explains that she came to know these ten individuals, and to work with them for *Exit – Entrance*, "by chance, all of them by chance. And all of them connected. I trust in my destiny."

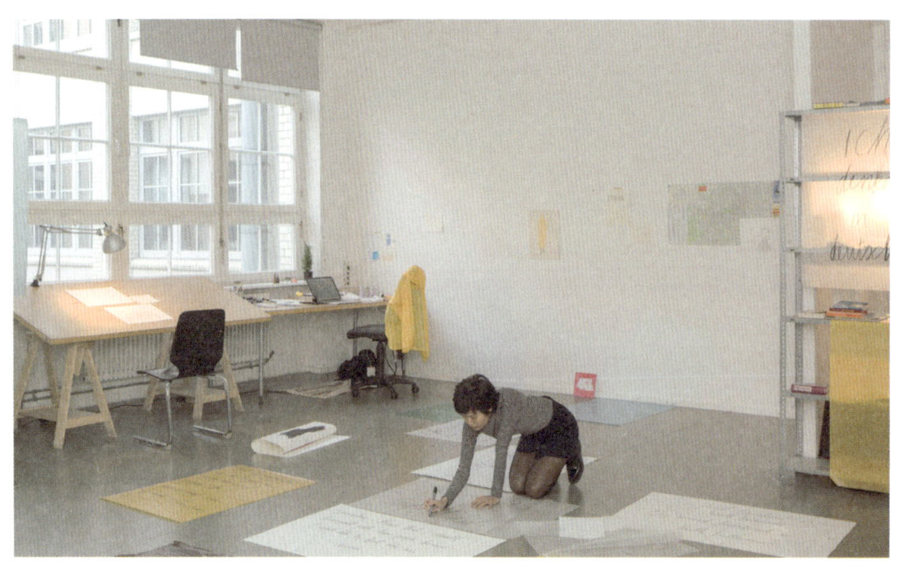

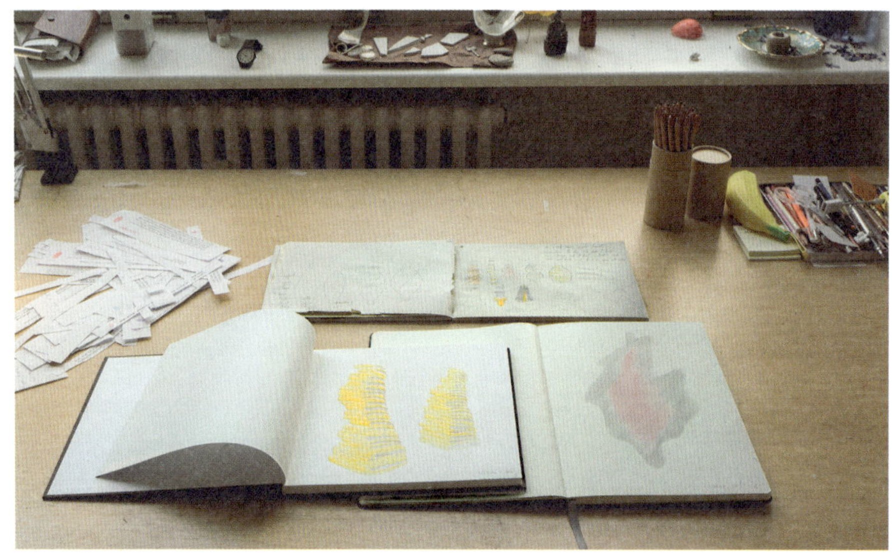

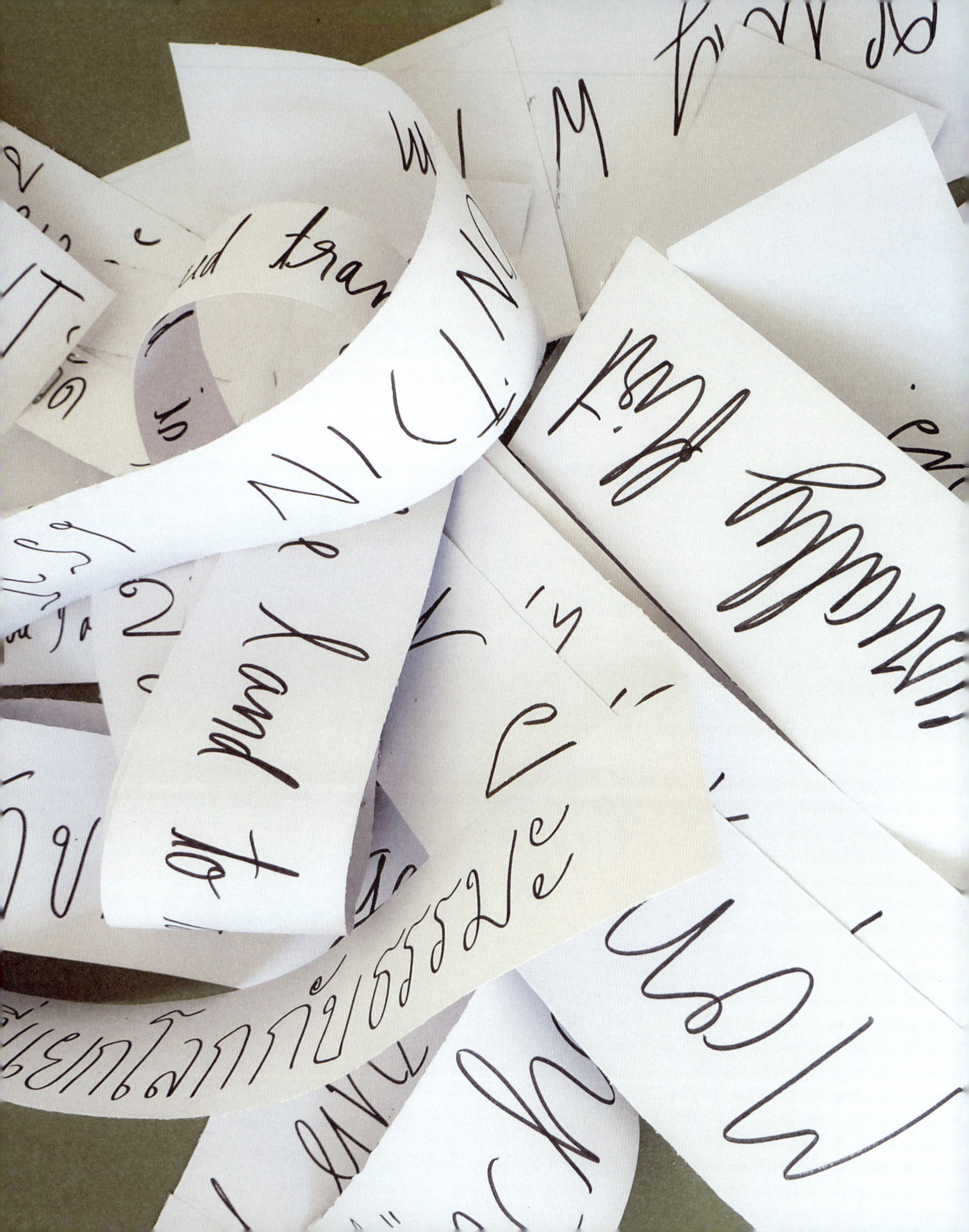

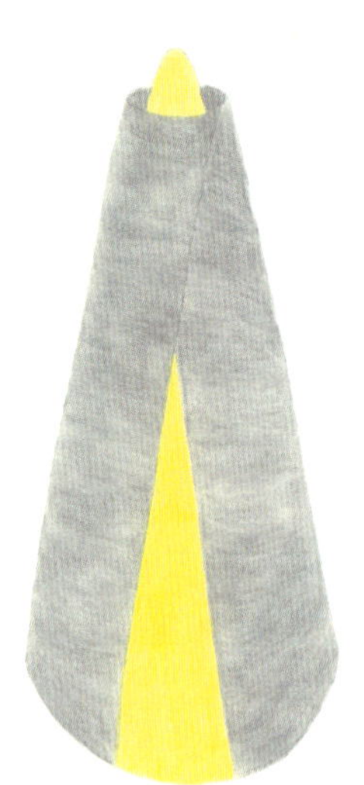

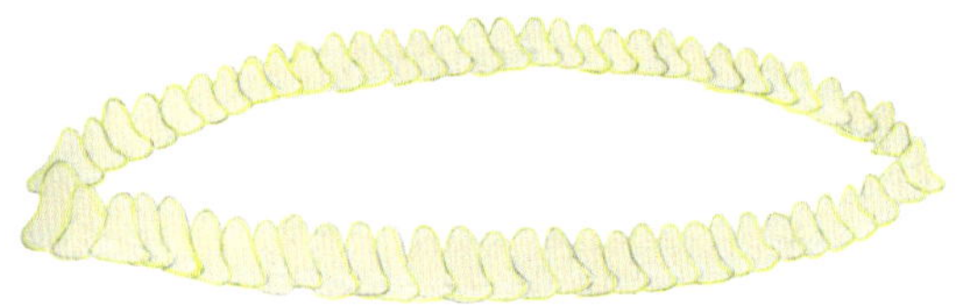
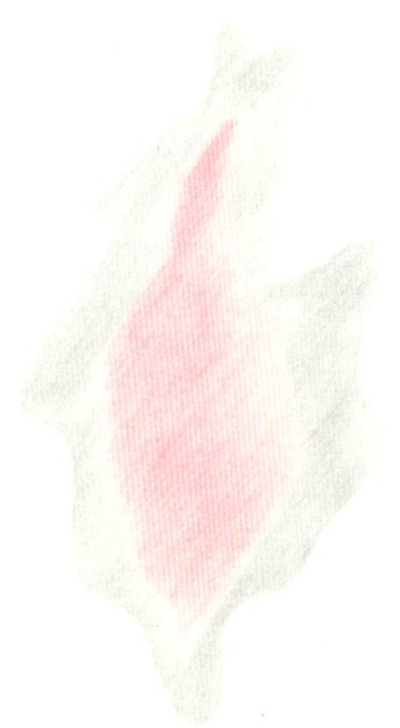
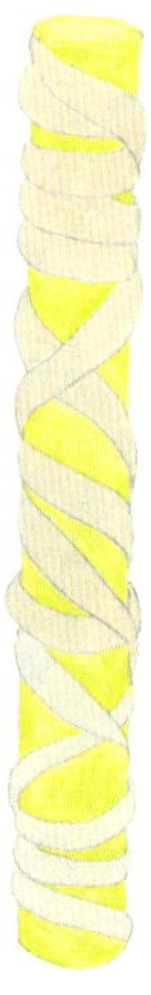

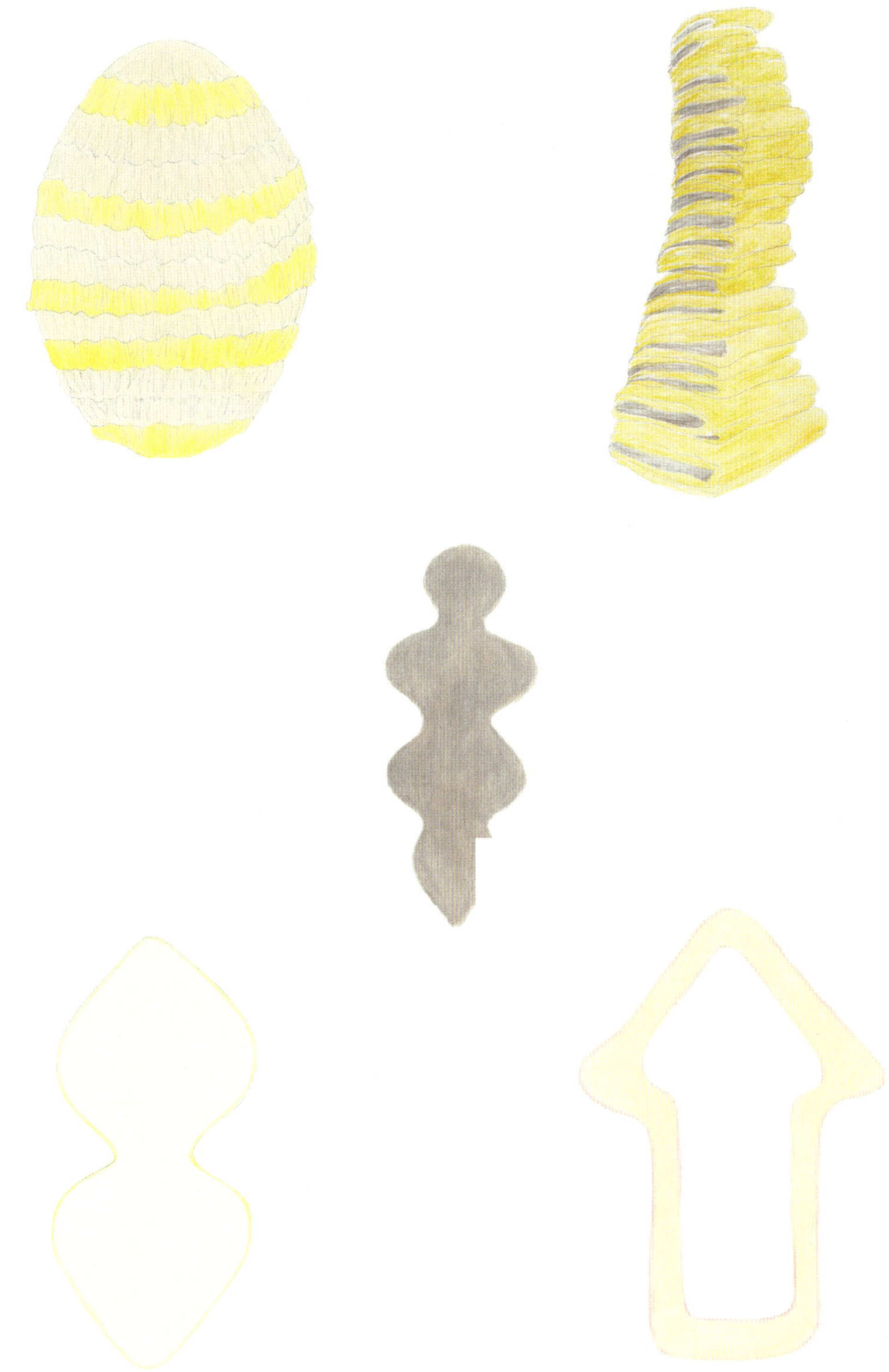

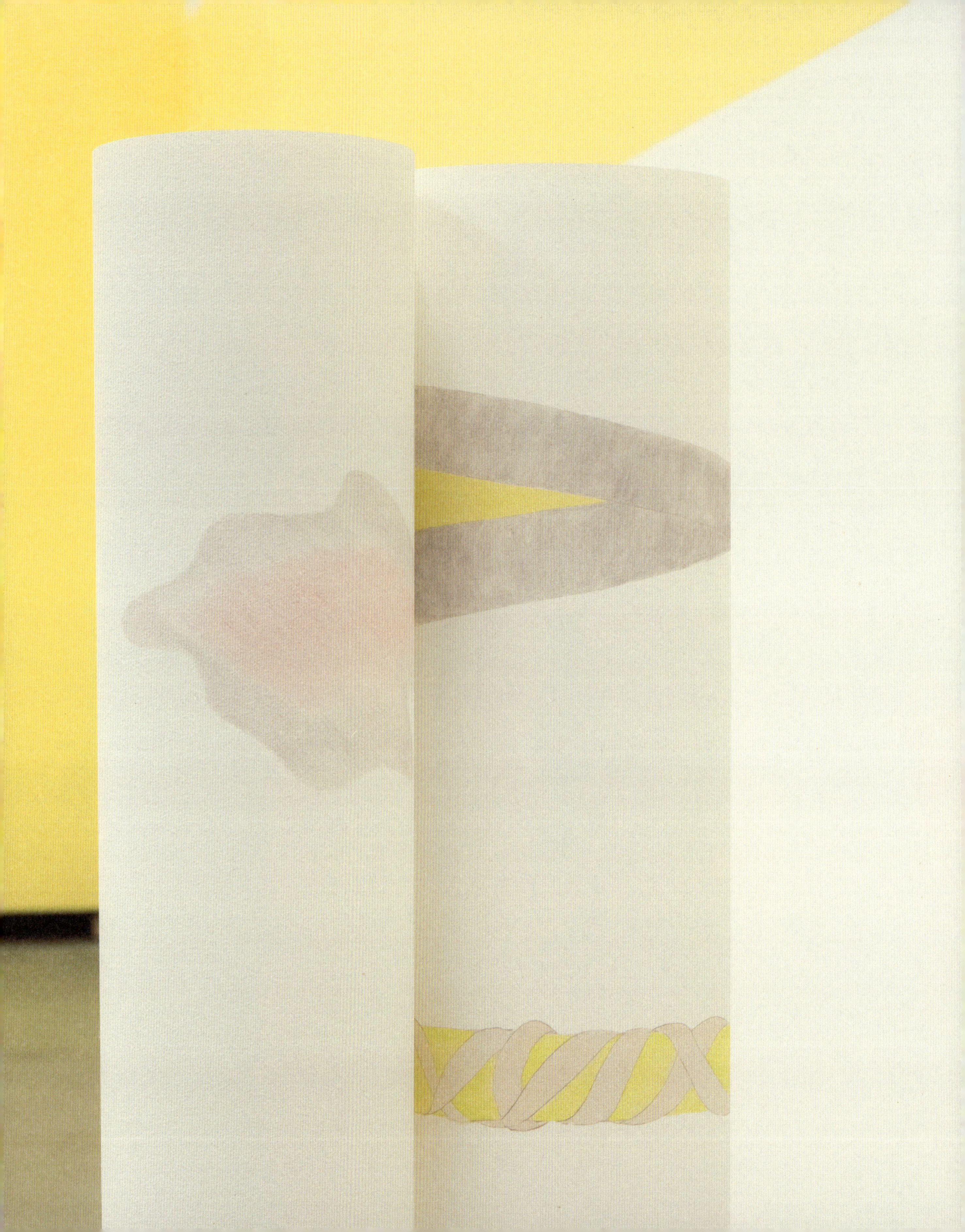

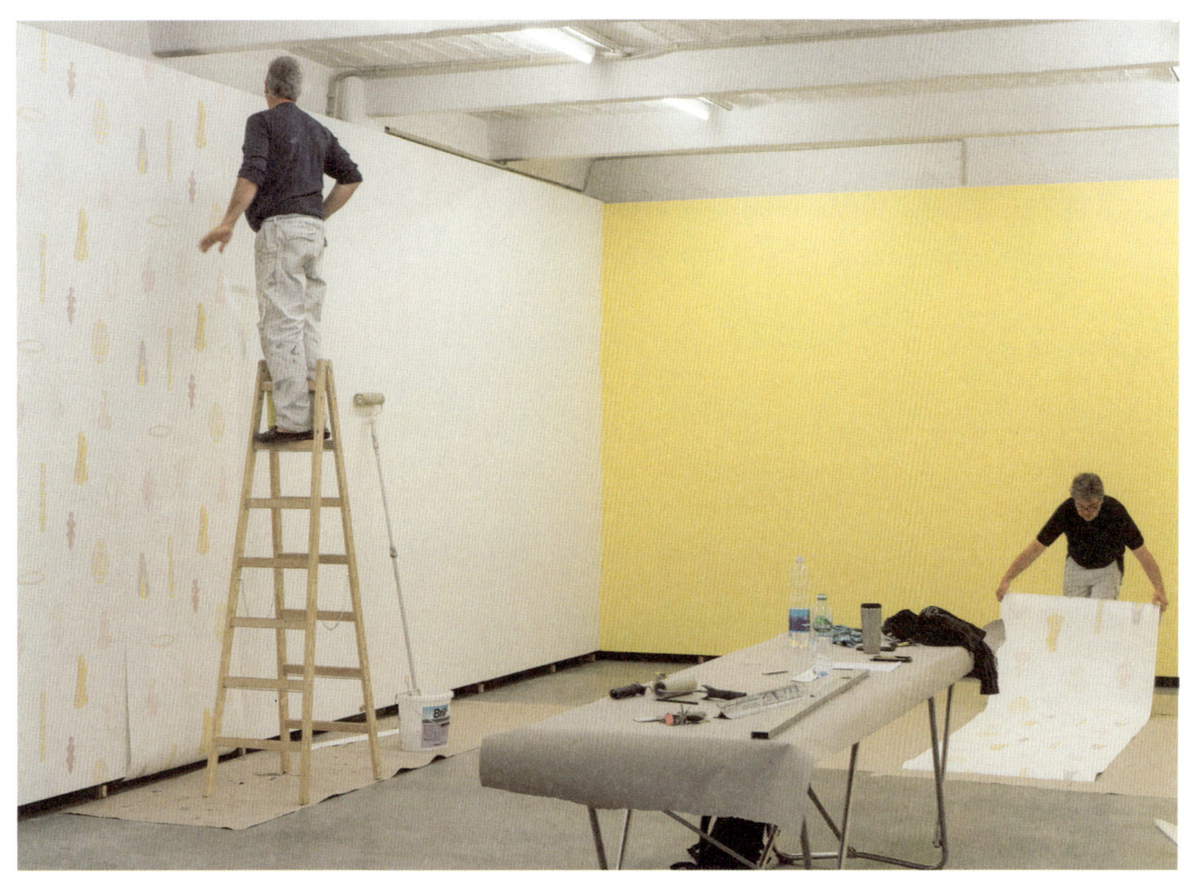

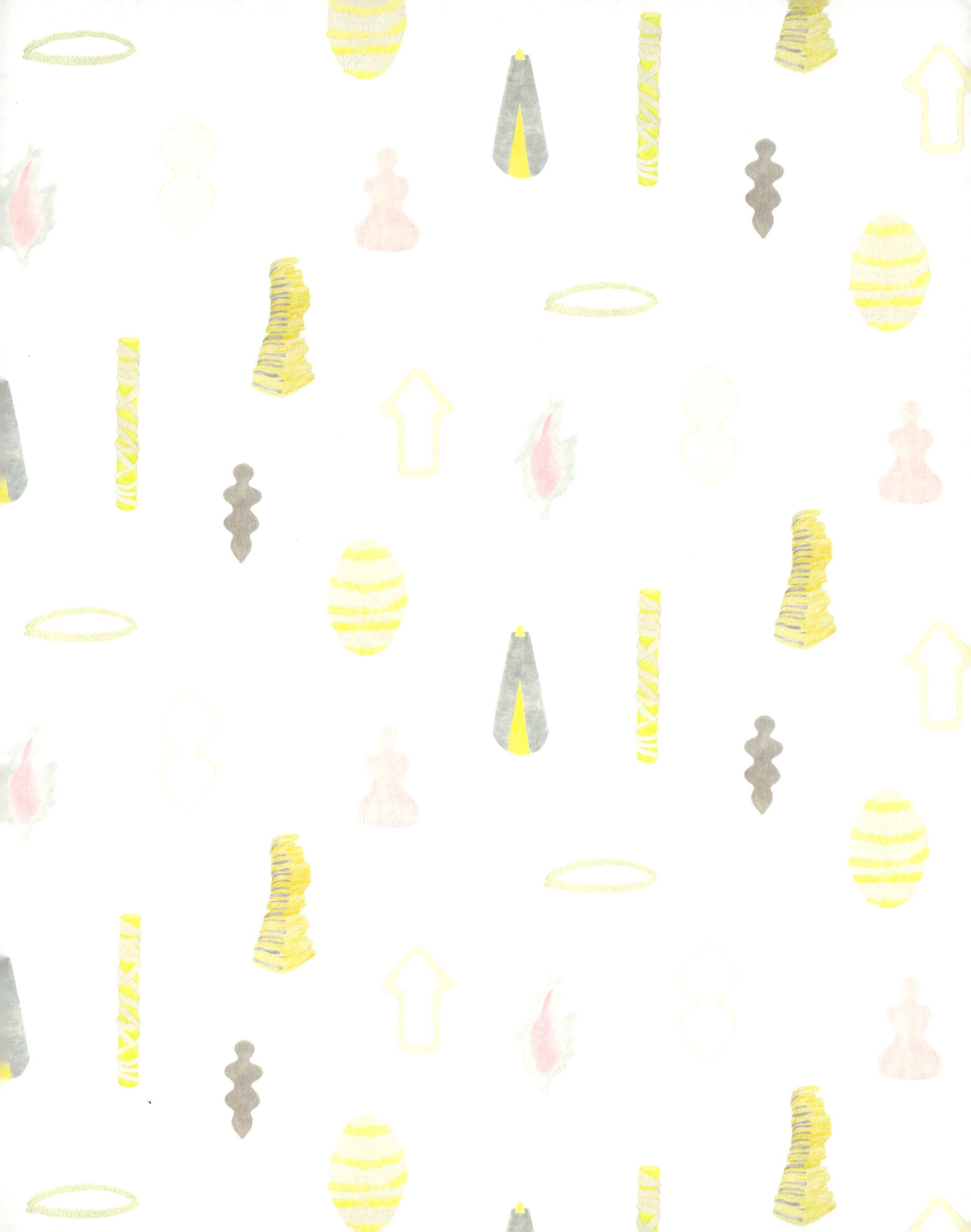

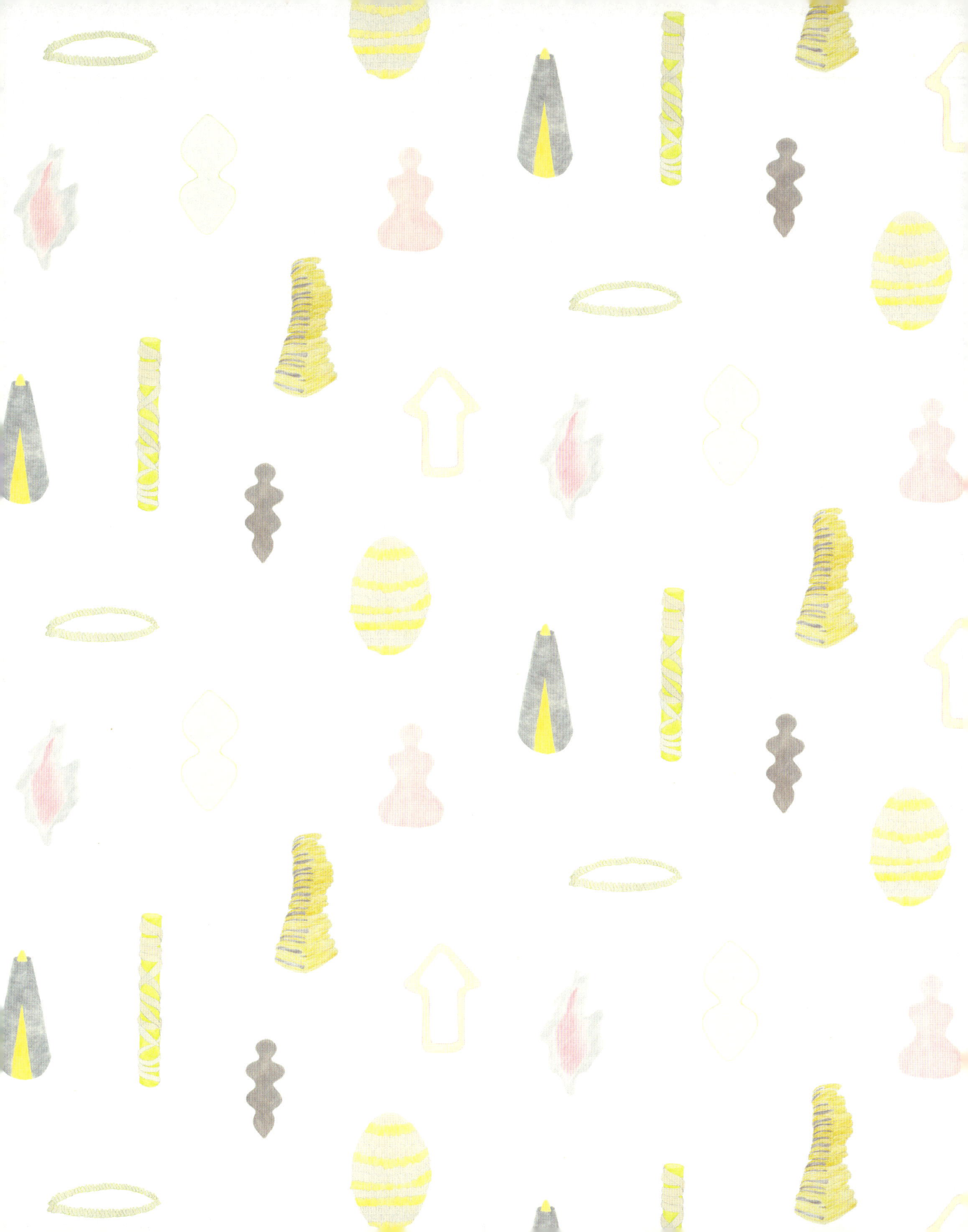

read and translate at home

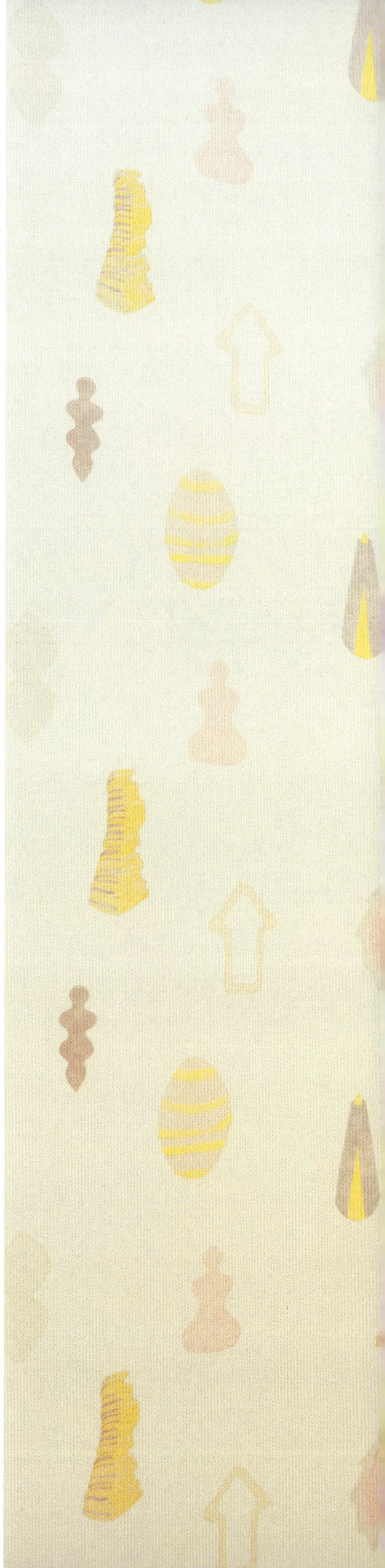

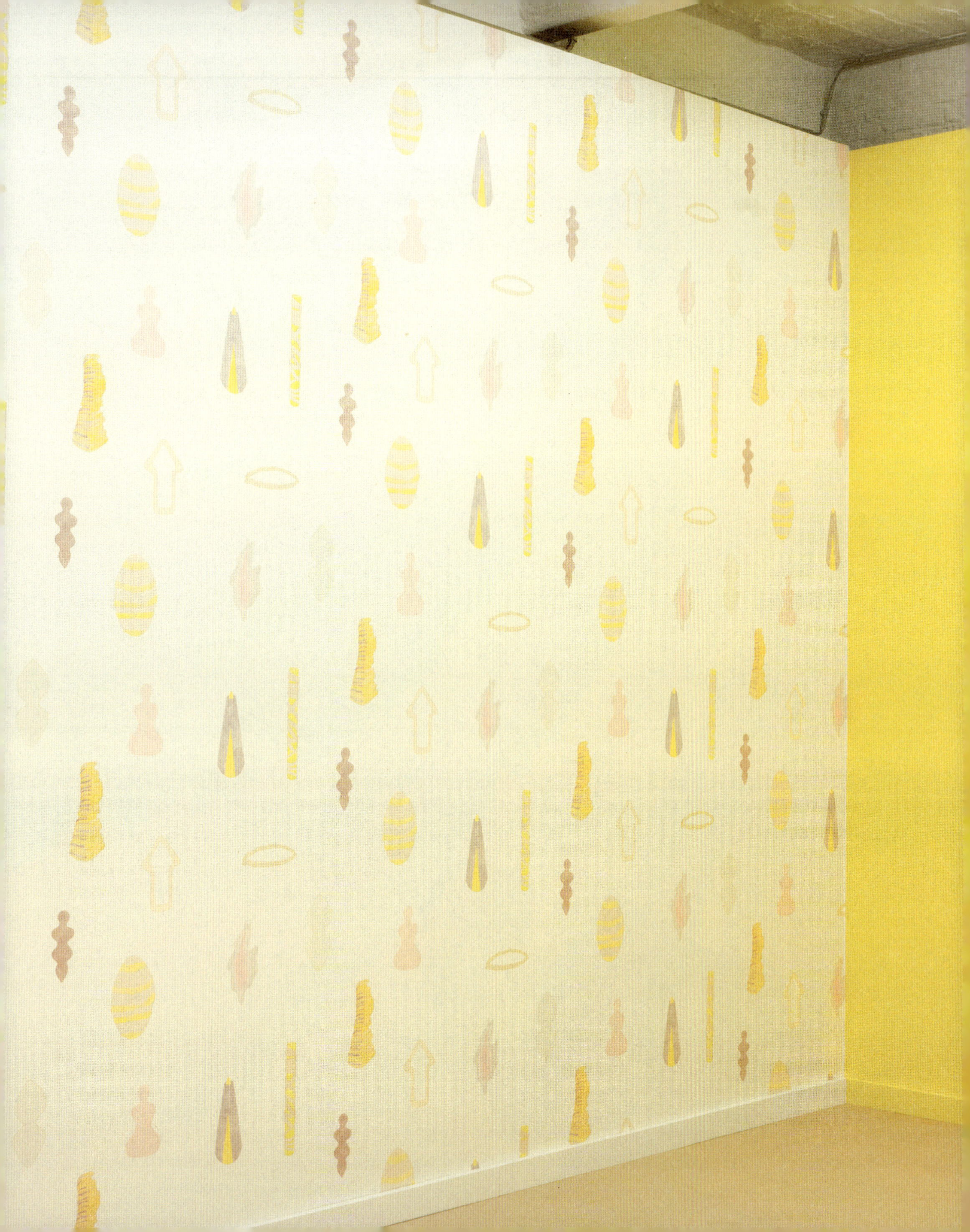

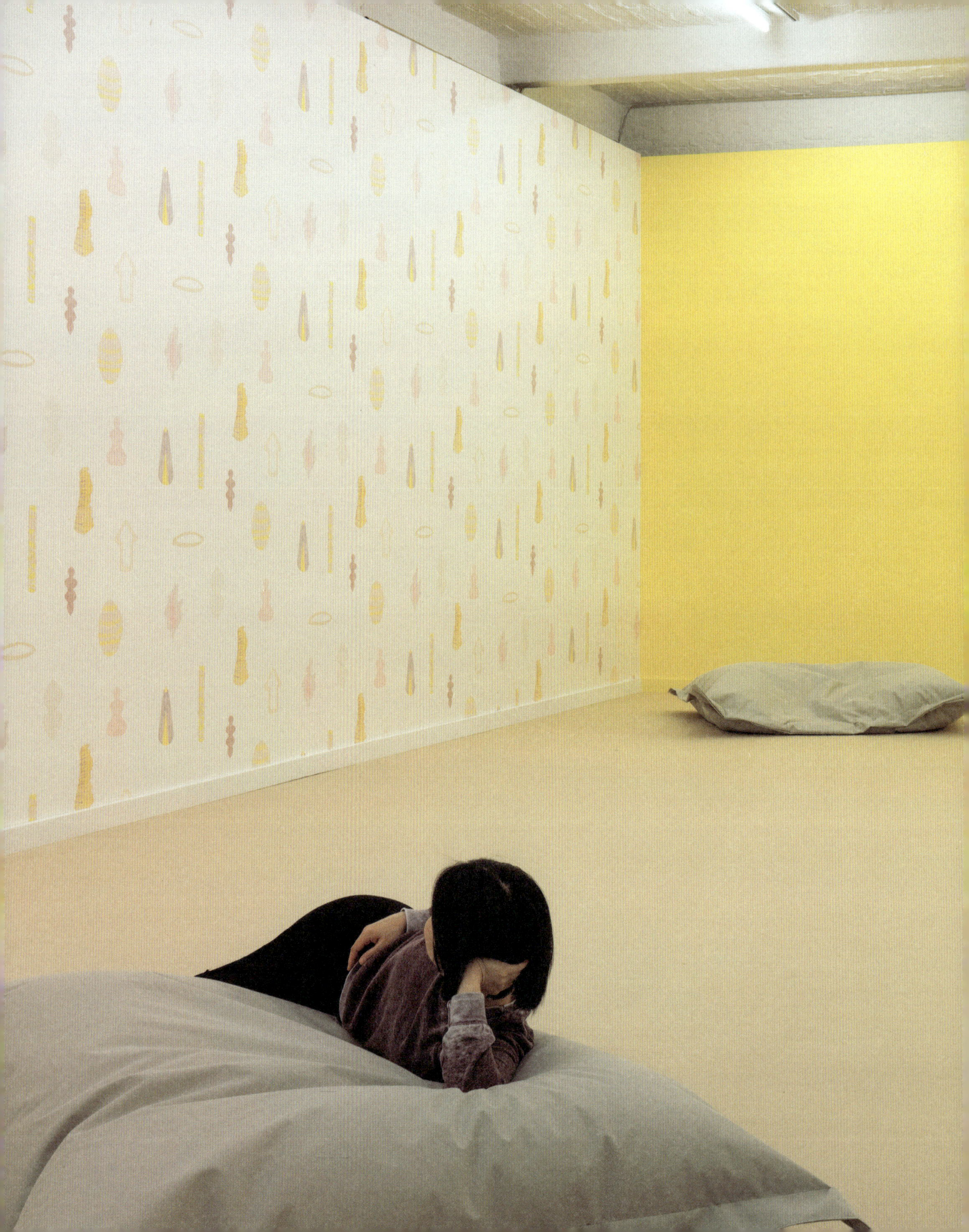

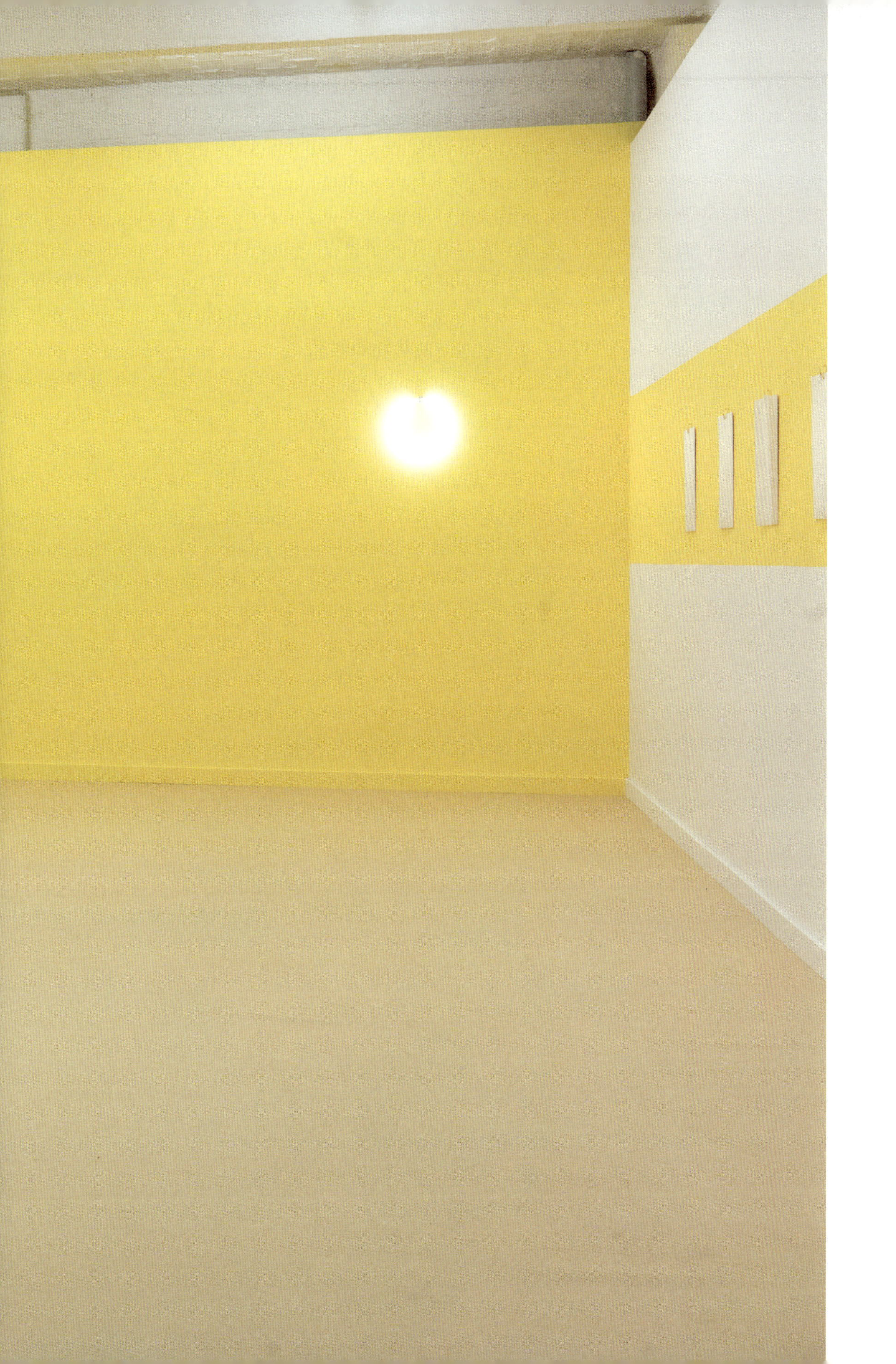

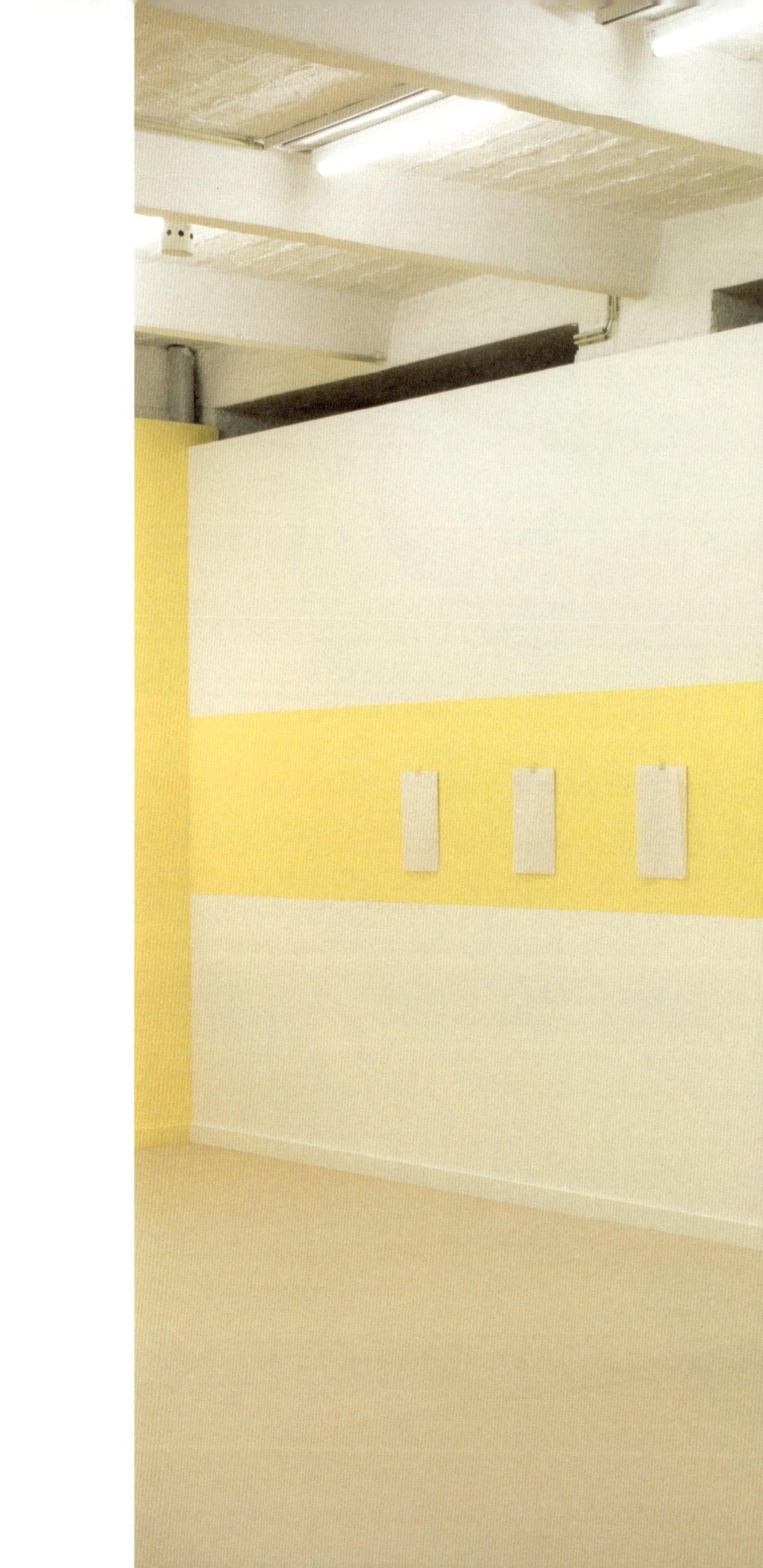

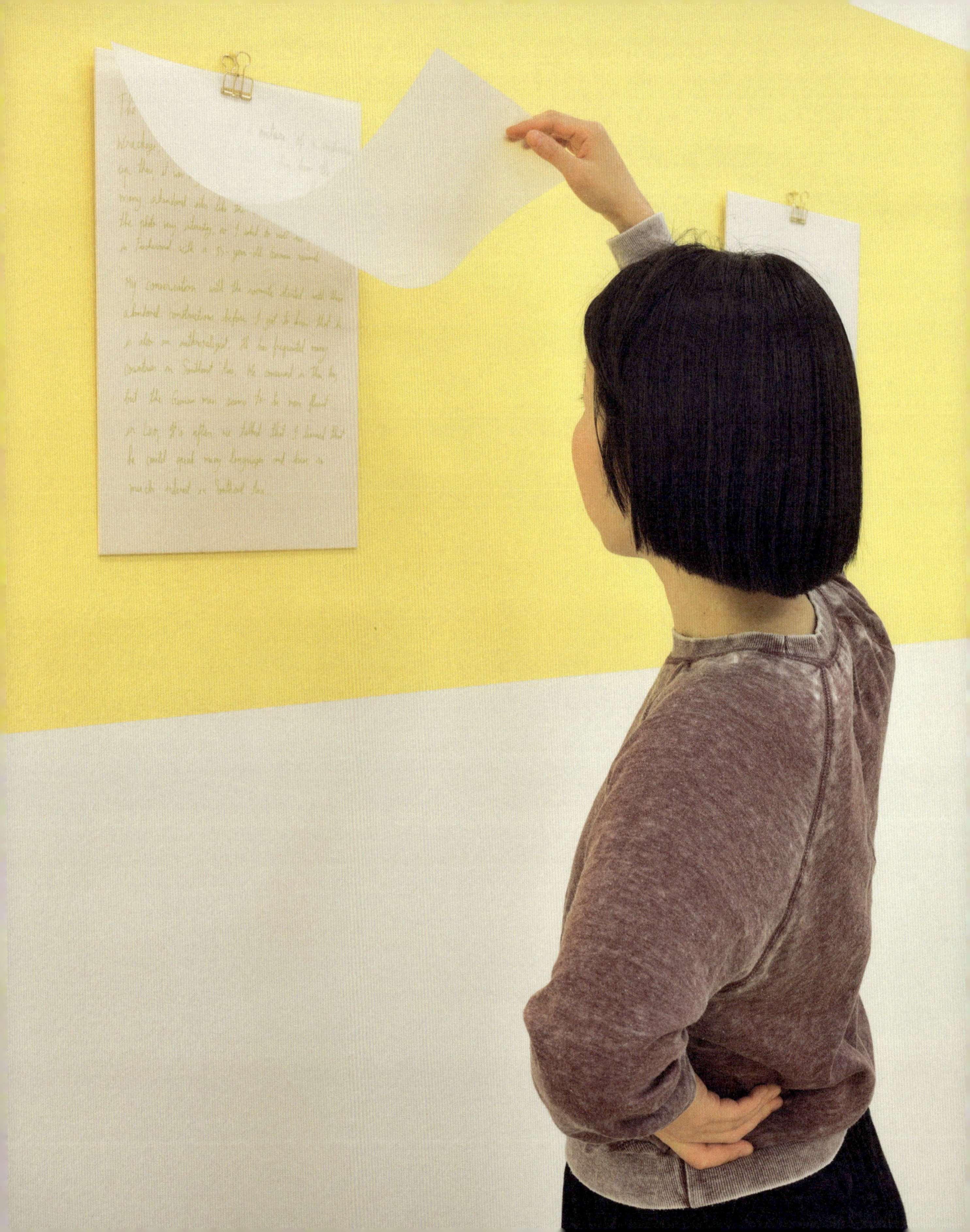

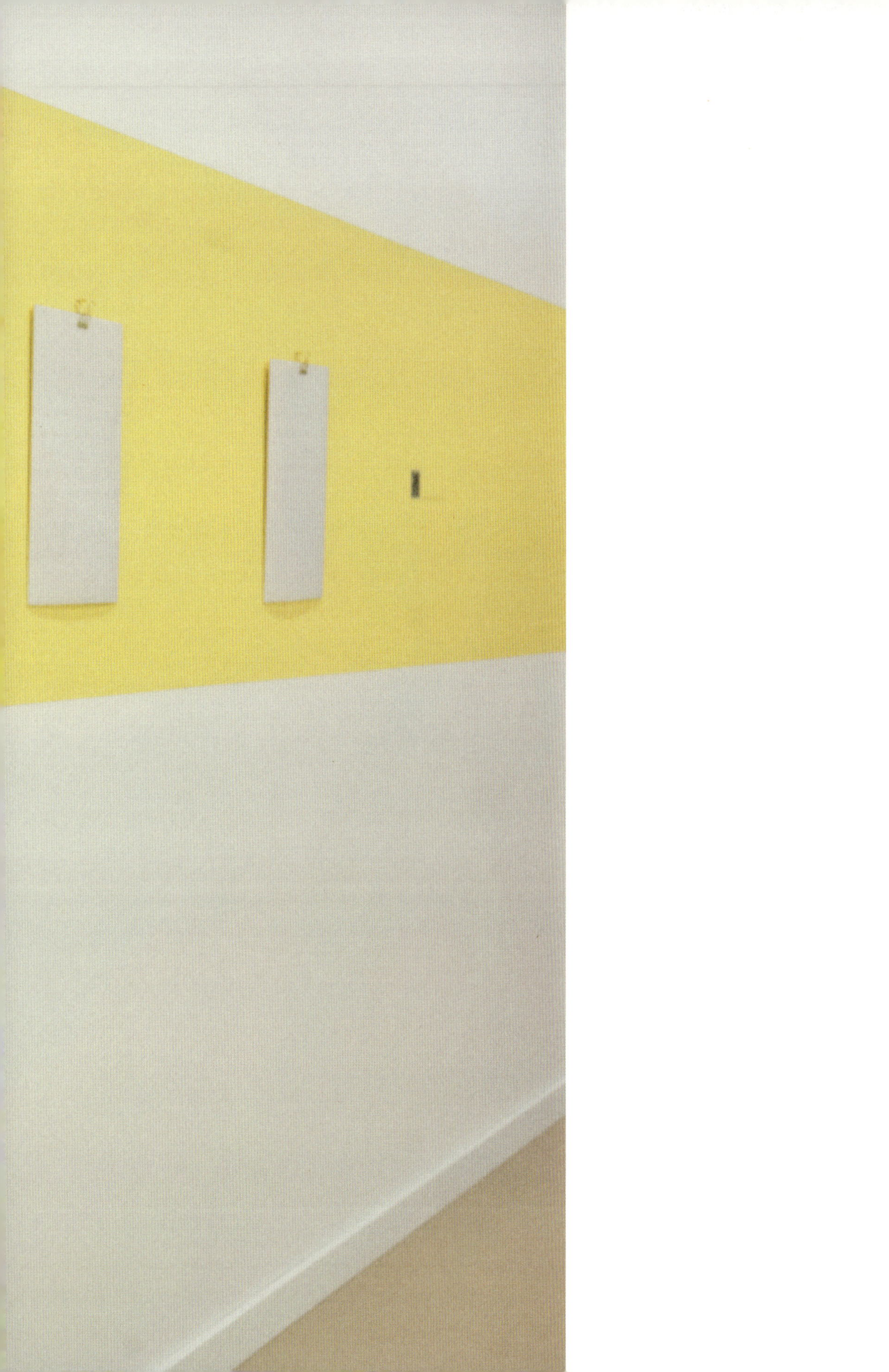

"I always wanted to be a local artist who reaches out to the world."

Orawan Arunrak in conversation with Yvette Mutumba

Yvette Mutumba (YM): What made you decide to become an artist, or more specifically, to study printmaking at the King Mongkut's Institute of Technology Ladkrabang in Bangkok? I am asking with regard to your more recent practice which deliberately excludes work with prints. What is the story behind your choice of medium – starting with printing and then moving on to drawing and installation?

Orawan Arunrak (OA): Since I was young I knew that I could only be an artist. I have always worked in the arts. That is the only way I know to earn money, mainly through jobs in art spaces and museums as an assistant curator. At the time, the university offered only three majors: sculpture, painting and printmaking. For me printmaking is a process, where you have to plan and prepare extensively. Because of that, printmaking prepared me to work with any other medium. All my artwork depends on a concept. I am not looking for one medium or to be an expert with one specific tool. Concept and content is more important to me.

YM: During 2014–2016, you travelled extensively to Cambodia, Vietnam, Sri Lanka as well as to Okinawa/Japan, Vientiane/Laos and to various regions in your home country Thailand. What was your motivation to travel to these different places?

OA: Firstly, instead of travelling I would rather say that I spent time in these places. I wanted to focus on possible connections between Asian cultures, but also to understand what I want to do in my artistic practice. I went to Cambodia and Vietnam at a time when not many other artists did that. At least not in the way I did it, going there, spending time, and slowly connecting with the local community. And I still go back regularly. So it really was not only about doing a residency or an exhibition, but also about finding another home. For me a residency is not only about a project. I rather try to put everything into it. So I am there completely. I feel at home, I like my bed, my desk, my room, and feel like they are mine. Then it comes down to the question: "Why am I here and where am I going?"

YM: What is your approach to finding answers to that question?

OA: In the beginning, I wanted to go to India to gain a better understanding of Asian culture. But India is very big and one would need quite a bit of time to get

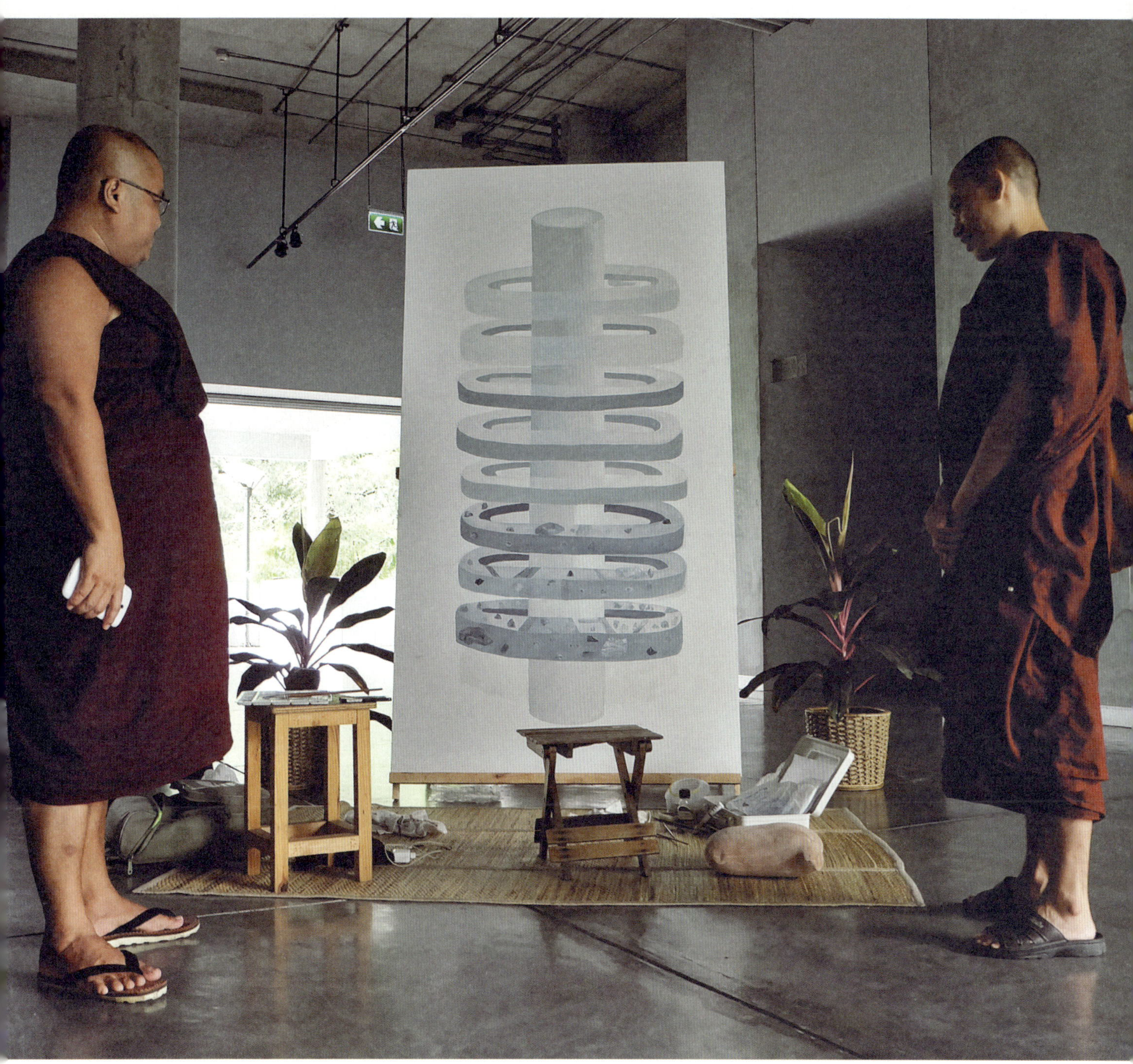

Meditating Painting, 2016

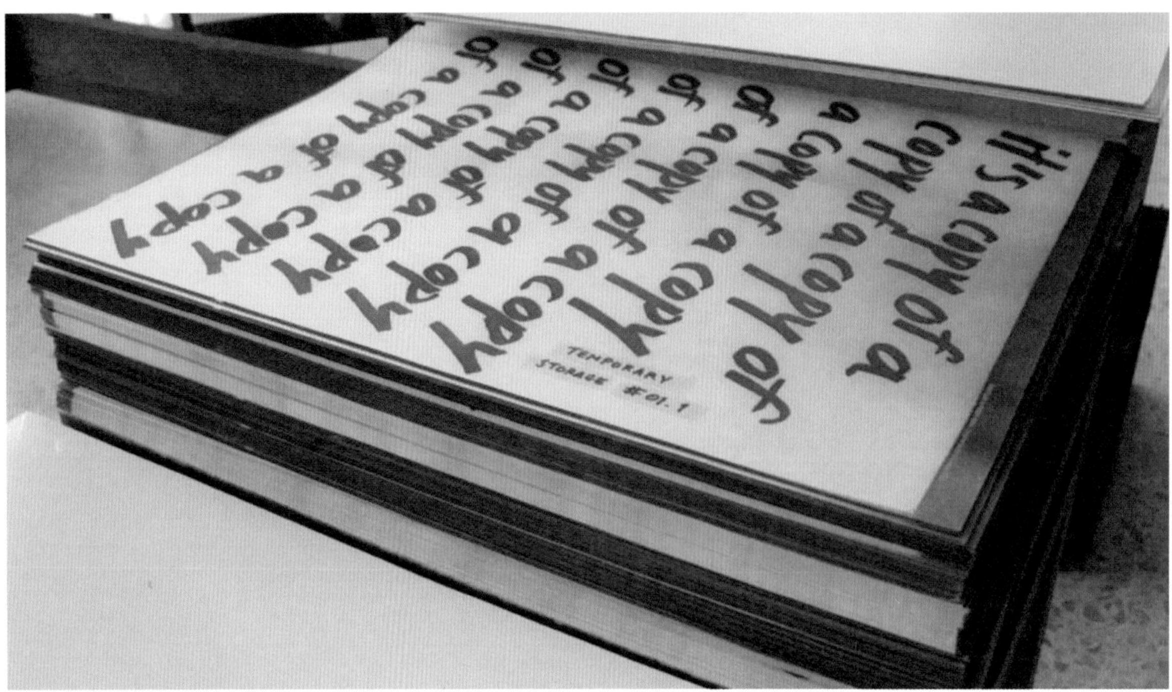

Drifting Map of Bangkok, 2012

there. Sri Lanka, however, is kind of in-between India and Asia. That is why I decided to go to Sri Lanka. This stay was not connected to an institution, but sponsored by a private collector. I was there by myself for around twenty days, just to spend time and do research, not necessarily to create work or to show the results in an exhibition. In Phnom Penh, I had the first "official" residency of my life, at Sa Sa Art Projects. For them it is really important to invite people not because of their CV, but because they feel it is someone who would connect with the city and be ready and interested to stay longer and get involved with the community. Actually, this kind of approach applies to all the institutions where I have done residencies.

I stayed in Phnom Penh for around two months and started to see connections between Thailand and Cambodia. When I talked to friends from Cambodia, the histories and presents came together. Sometimes, it was just little everyday things. For example, when we would sit in a restaurant we would see objects from Vietnam that we all knew, things like the ketchup. And it became a joke. In Thailand, I did not see these connections. We Thai people tend to look down on our neighbours and therefore do not really see or talk about these connections. But in Cambodia it came really naturally. After that I thought it would make sense to stay in Vietnam.

YM: Once you realised that there are connections more questions must have come up?

OA: The Cambodian and Vietnamese histories are really painful compared with the Thai history. Of course we also have many painful histories, but they remain kind of hidden. We hardly talk about them. This is why we call Thailand "the land of smile" and that is why many

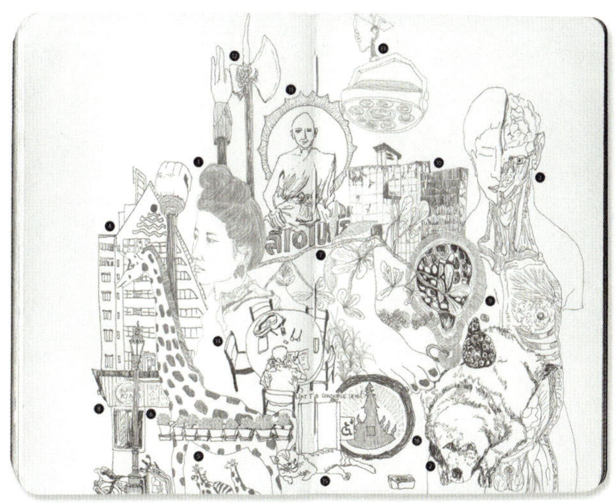

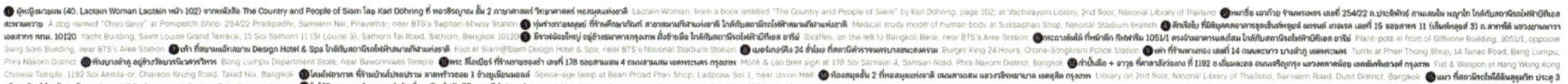

1 Laotain Woman, from a book entitled "The Country and People of Siam" by Karl Döhring, page 102; at Vachirayarn Library, 2nd floor, National Library of Thailand 2 A dog named "Chao Gauy" at Pompetch Shop, 254/22 Pradipadhi, Samsern Nai, Phayathai; near BTS's Saphan-Khway Station 3 Medical study model of human body at Suksaphan Shop, National Stadium branch 4 Yachi Building, Saint Louise Grand Terrace, 15 Soi Sathorn 11 (St Louise 3), Sathorn Tai Road, Sathorn, Bangkok 10120 5 Giraffes, on the left to Bangkok Bank, near BTS's Aree Station 6 Plant-pots in front of Gifferine Building, 1051/1, opposite Sang Som Building, near BTS's Aree Station 7 Foot at Siam@Siam Design Hotel & Spa, near BTS's National Stadium Station 8 Burger King 24 Hours, Chana-Songkram Police Station 9 Turtle at Phan Thong Shop, 14 Tanao Road, Bang Lumpu, Phra Nakorn District 10 Bang Lumpu Department Store, near Bawonniwes Temple 11 Monk & Lao Beer sign at 178 Soi Samsen 4, Samsen Road, Phra Nakorn District, Bangkok 12 Fist & Weapon at Hang Wong Kong Chinese Temple, 1192 Soi Aemla-or, Charoen Krung Road, Talad Noi, Bangkok 13 Space-age lamp at Baan Proad Pran Shop, Ladprao Soi 1, near Union Mall 14 Library on 2nd floor, National Library of Thailand, Samsern Road, Dusit District, Bangkok 15 Cat at MRT's Sukhumvit Station, Exit #3, near elevator 16 Logo of Phra Nakorn Co-operative Store Limited, Exit #4 of BTS's Aree Station

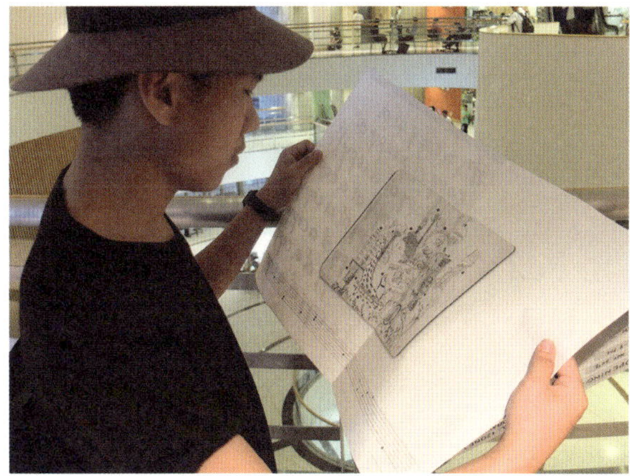

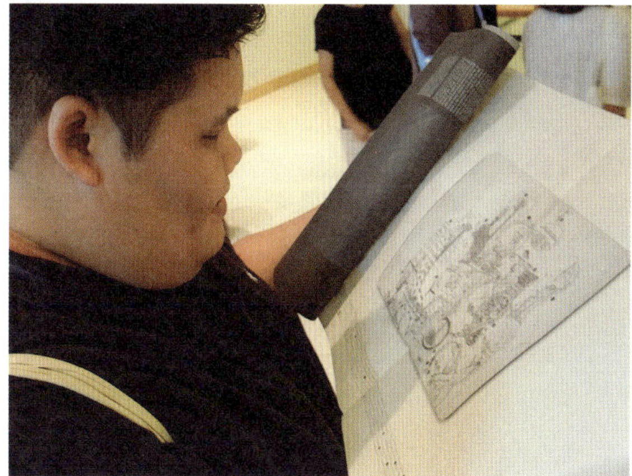

Drifting Map of Bangkok, 2012

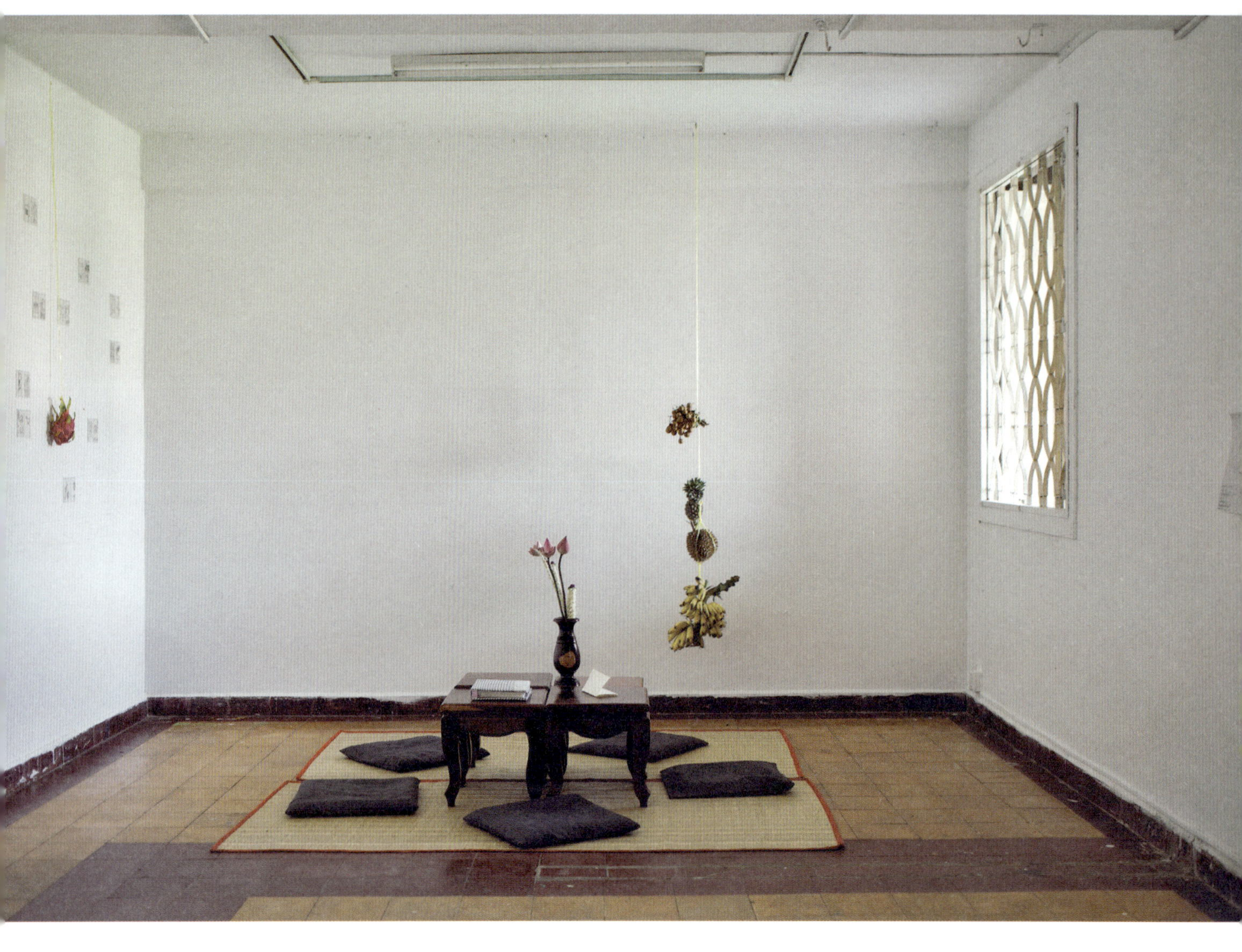

Come In, 2014

people think we are always happy. Cambodian and Vietnamese friends would say: "Oh, I am really happy to have you here, because you are from an entertainment country". Hearing that, I would feel a bit ashamed and curious at the same time. It is of course nice to make people happy, but rather behind the scenes and not as a label. So I wanted to know the connections and understand why I have to entertain. I also needed to understand this in order to know who I am. Because of that, I started to see that my country can be viewed from many perspectives.

YM: How did that discovery influence your artistic practice?

OA: To answer that, I first have to go back a bit: After I graduated, I started a job at the Bangkok Art and Culture Centre (BACC). It is a big space in the centre of the city. Often people would get lost and ask what was happening there. I was really excited, because I had just graduated and wanted to tell people what art was. In Thailand, contemporary art is kind of new. I had to explain to them what it was. They would know a painting from inside a temple, or a sculpture outside a bank, but it was different to see a painting in a gallery. I also had to explain how to move in the gallery: please go upstairs, please leave your bag, please don't touch that. It was really back to zero. This was an important, refreshing time for me. I enjoyed it. This was also a time to practice, to understand and to get to know the art system. But after one year, I started to think about what my artistic practice could be without thinking about money, without having a studio. It was not easy for me to get back into producing art. It might seem like you can just jump back into it any time. But actually for me that is not the case. I have to practice. It is like doing homework. To keep practicing I promised myself to have a solo exhibition each year. Not in order to have it on my CV, but to constantly train my brain, reflect on my work, to see how the audience reacts and thinks about it.

When I worked at the BACC I decided to work with the simple medium of a sketchbook and a pencil. In my breaks, I would go outside and draw places that people were sort of missing because they would just look at their iPhone. And I was concerned about the audience. I wanted them to spend time in the exhibition space, to get to know art better. So my work from that time onward was about sharing the inside and the outside of the museum. My own drawings could be seen outside. In that way I tried to create a relationship between the museum and the city. So it was in Bangkok that I started to walk outside in the streets.

In Cambodia, I continued this practice – walking in the streets and drawing. I wanted to meet people through that. Sa Sa Art Projects had a space for the artists in residency to work with the community. So I wanted to initiate something. I had passed by a building many times and had drawn it. Now I wanted to get in touch with the people living inside. I started to draw my face, not completely realistically though, to introduce myself. I would write in Cambodian: "I would like to draw your house and if you are interested please call me". For one week no one called me of course. So I started drawing outside. Many people would come to watch. That was my chance. I would ask them: "Can I come to your place?" And they would say: "Yes, you are not a stranger anymore". Then I went to their house and made sketches of their room. While I was drawing, we would have conversations. They would talk a lot. And my drawings became a kind of writing.

I would draw in the same size like photos in a photo album. At the end of my residency, I invited the community to come to see my project, only for one day. We sat together and looked at the fifteen photo albums I had made (*Come In, 2014*). In contrast to a photo, which would have been a clear image of a private space, the drawings gave a less specific idea of the rooms I had visited. In that way neighbours would get to know each other without having to completely disclose their pri-

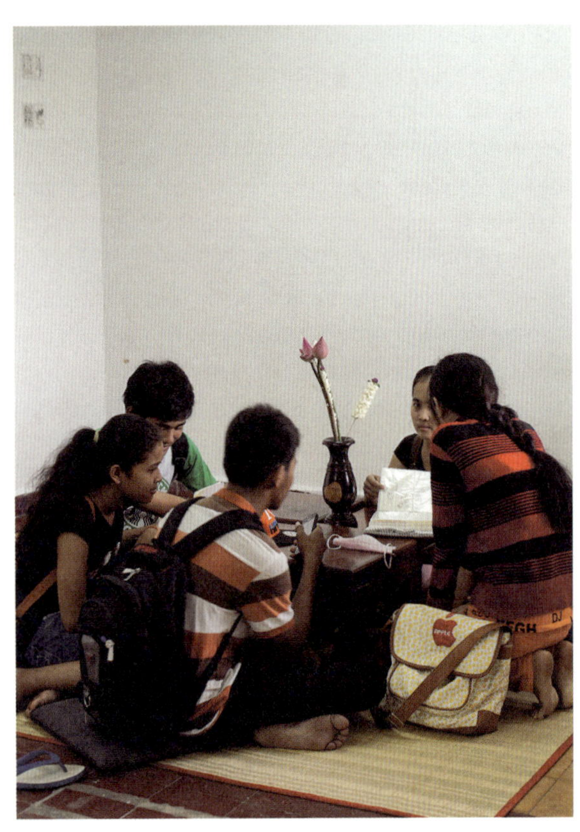

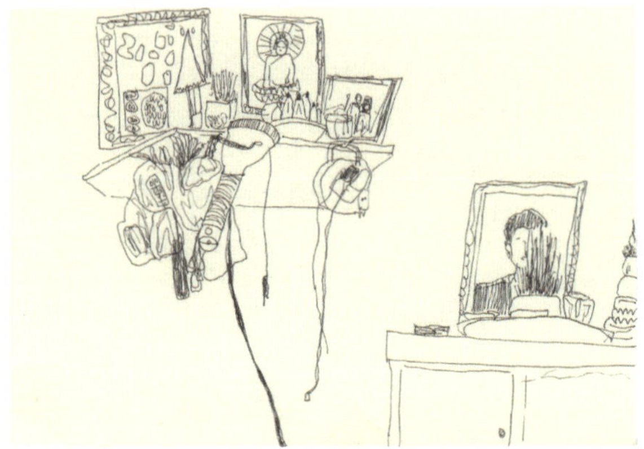

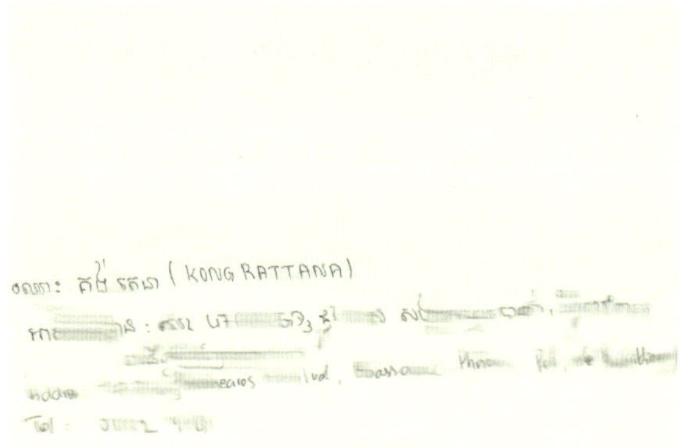
(KONG RATTANA)

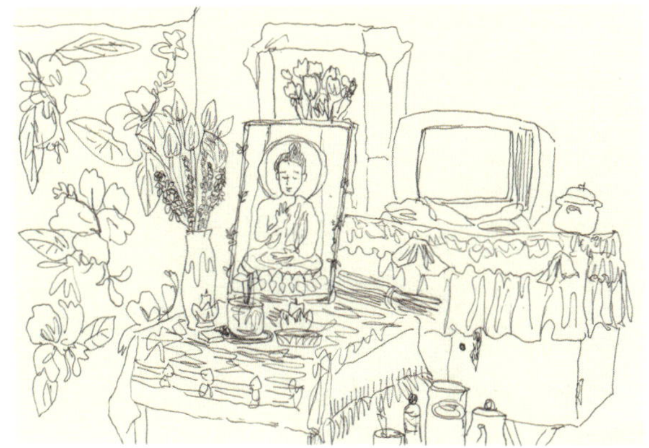

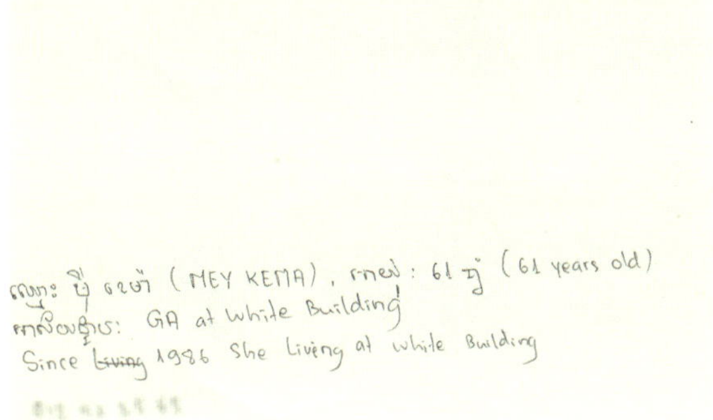
(MEY KEMA)
61 (61 years old)
GA at White Building
Since ~~Living~~ 1986 She Living at White Building

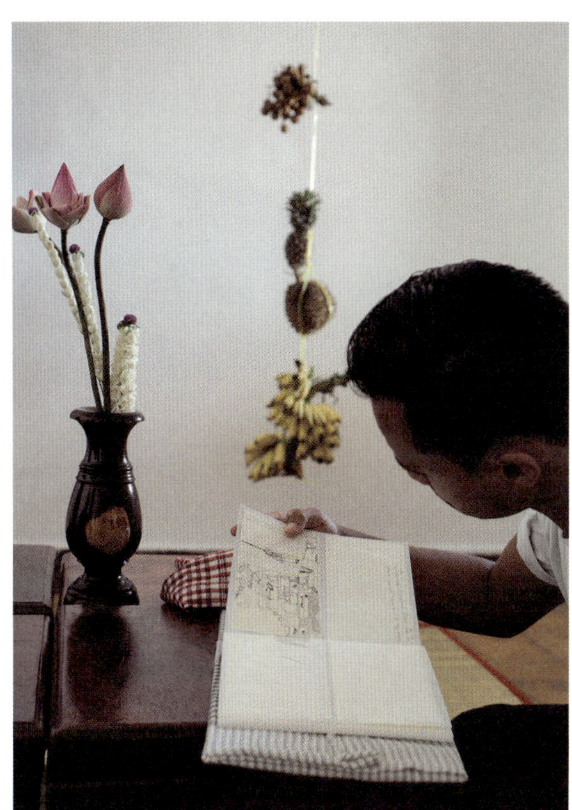

Come In, 2014

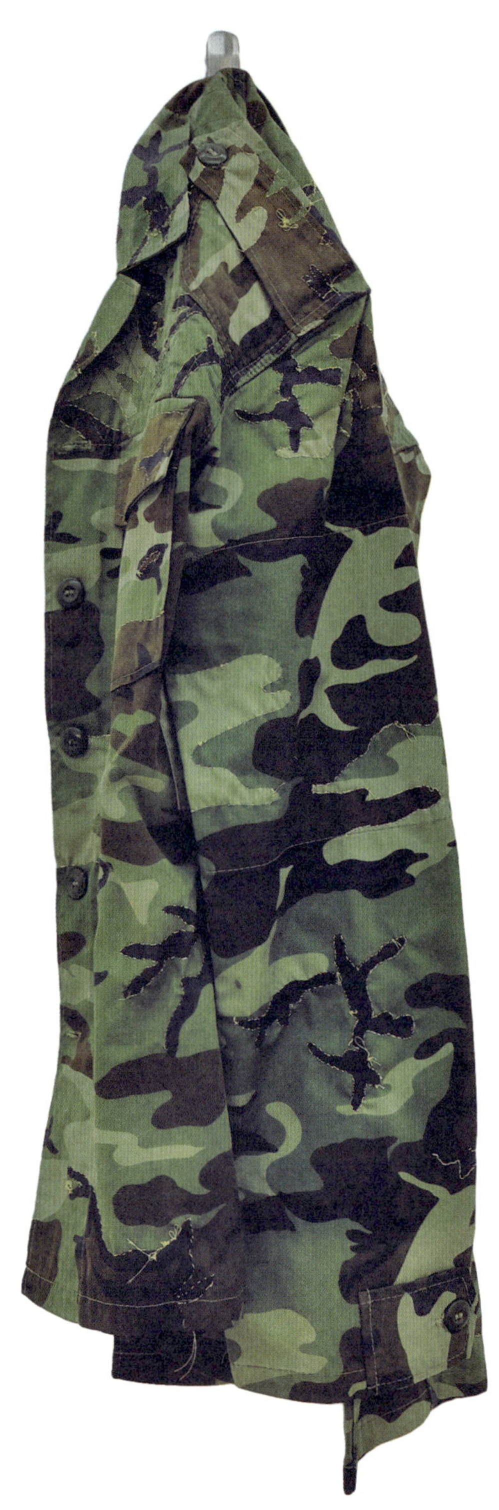

My Godfather, 2014–15

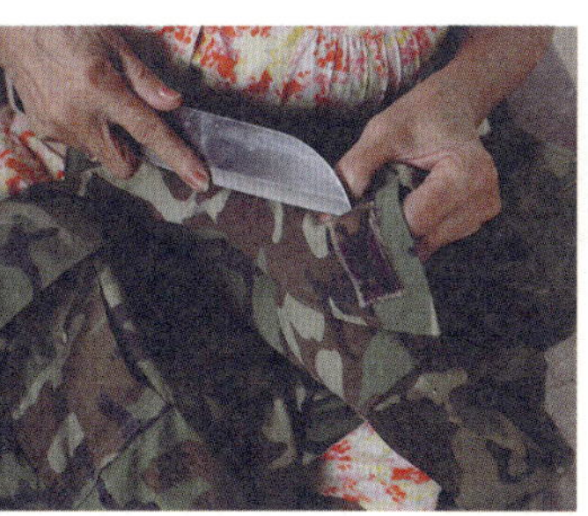
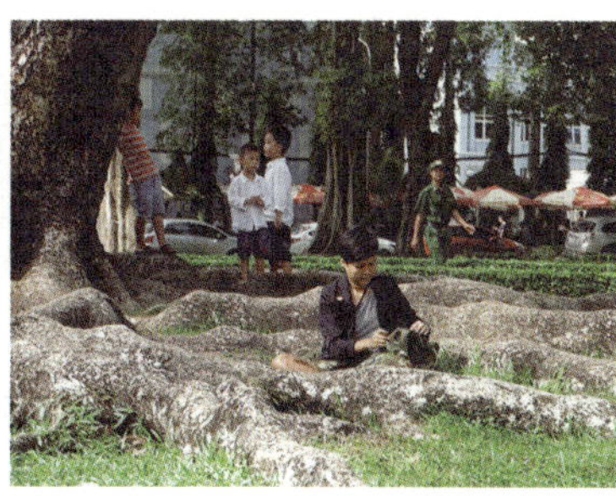
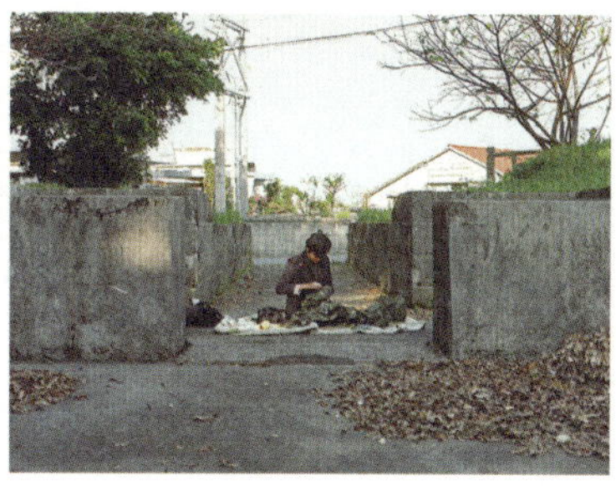
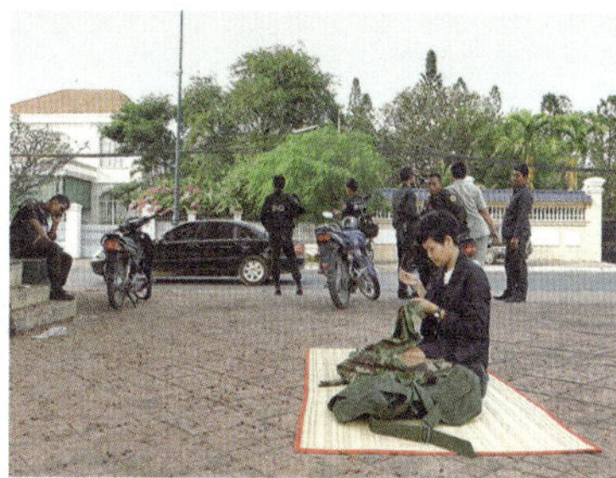

My Godfather: She Preserves Godfather's Dignity (left), *War Journey*, Phnom Penh, Okinawa, Ho Chi Minh City (next 3 images), 2014–15

vacy. Often they had lived next to each other for years and had never talked to each other. Now they started to have conversations.

YM: When you were visiting those people what would they be talking about?

OA: It depends. One woman was practicing traditional dance, so she would show me her dance routines. I also spent time with a lonely wife who told me that she had been fighting with her husband the other day. So some would tell me really private things.

YM: It is quite special that they trusted you so quickly.

OA: Yes, I was sitting in these small rooms and felt like I was a new member of the family. But as I was a stranger it may have been easier. It is easier to tell secrets to a stranger, thinking that this person will never come back, so the secret is safe. When I finished the project and passed by that building looking at the windows, I would think: "Oh, I do know some secrets that are inside that building ..." They stayed in my head. I never made those secrets part of my work. I just wanted people to come and talk to each other. I had also made installations with different pieces of furniture and a carpet that resembled those in the rooms. In that way a broader audience could get a more physical idea of these rooms.

While I was drawing buildings only from the outside in Bangkok, this project in Cambodia was the next step by going inside. It was my chance to get to know people in a new city where I didn't know anyone.

YM: What did you personally take out of that after hearing all these stories?

OA: It was a change that came step by step. Phnom Penh was a new city, still Cambodia was somehow "same same but different". I realised that we have the same roots. I could see similarities for example in the decoration of the rooms I visited. But I still really focussed on the conversations. After Cambodia, when I went to Vietnam, I became more curious about the broader history.

YM: How did you make that next step of looking further into social and historical issues?

OA: It is important to say that between Cambodia and Vietnam I went back home. I grew up with a godmother, who is not actually my mother. At that time my godfather had just passed away. My mother kept talking a lot about her husband. At some point I asked her to tell me more about his work as I realised that I did not really know what he had done. So I asked her this stupid question: "Why is our family still poor?" She replied: "Because your dad forgot to take the gold from the refugees." And I said: "Oh, well, you have to please give me more information on this ..."

My home town is close to the Cambodian border. I learned that my godfather had been a soldier to protect Cambodian refugees along the Thai border during the 1980s. I was never really interested in this before. Everywhere in the world there are problems along borders. I asked my mother to give me his military jacket. Before she did that, she removed the name and identification from it. The resulting forms looked like a map to me. I used it for an art piece by doing performances with it in different public spaces in Bangkok, Vietnam, India and Japan (*My Godfather*, 2014–15).

YM: As you described that these countries are so close together, do people go there or do they prefer to travel further?

OA: Well, I can only give examples. At the time I was there my Cambodian friends would only travel via YouTube ... But more recently, they would save money or get scholarships to really travel. Some of them actually speak Thai. Normally, you would think they would want to learn Mandarin or Cantonese, which are more useful languages. But Cambodian people want to learn Thai because of the soap operas. That is why they call Thailand an entertainment country ... TV and the internet mainly influence this. In reverse, Thai people in the past, if they had money, wanted to travel to Singapore or Japan. But more recently, maybe for three years now, they have also started to travel to Cambodia and Vietnam.

YM: Because Cambodia and Vietnam have a new coolness factor?

OA: Yes, mainly because of social media. People are more connected and have a better idea of their neighbouring countries through images on Facebook, Instagram etc. Of course that applies to anyone in the world. Additionally, it has become more affordable. If you fly from Saigon to Hanoi for example, it is the same price like going to Bangkok. Just right now Thai people are starting to realise that they can actually afford the big star hotels in Vietnam. This mainly applies to the middle class but also working class people can travel these days because of promotions and information on how to travel cheaply.

YM: I would like to go back to the idea of you being in these different contexts. In a way this also has an anthropological aspect. Like an anthropologist you go to foreign places to understand them. Often, speaking from a European perspective now, it is a researcher from the "West" entering the "other", the "non-Western" society to record and to understand it. Obviously you are not an anthropologist, but you also work in foreign contexts. But it is not about finding out the differences, but to actually find out how close you are to the people you meet. I was wondering whether you ever thought about this. Also because it is interesting how people would open up to you so easily. Hence you know of stories that a scientific researcher would never hear. In that

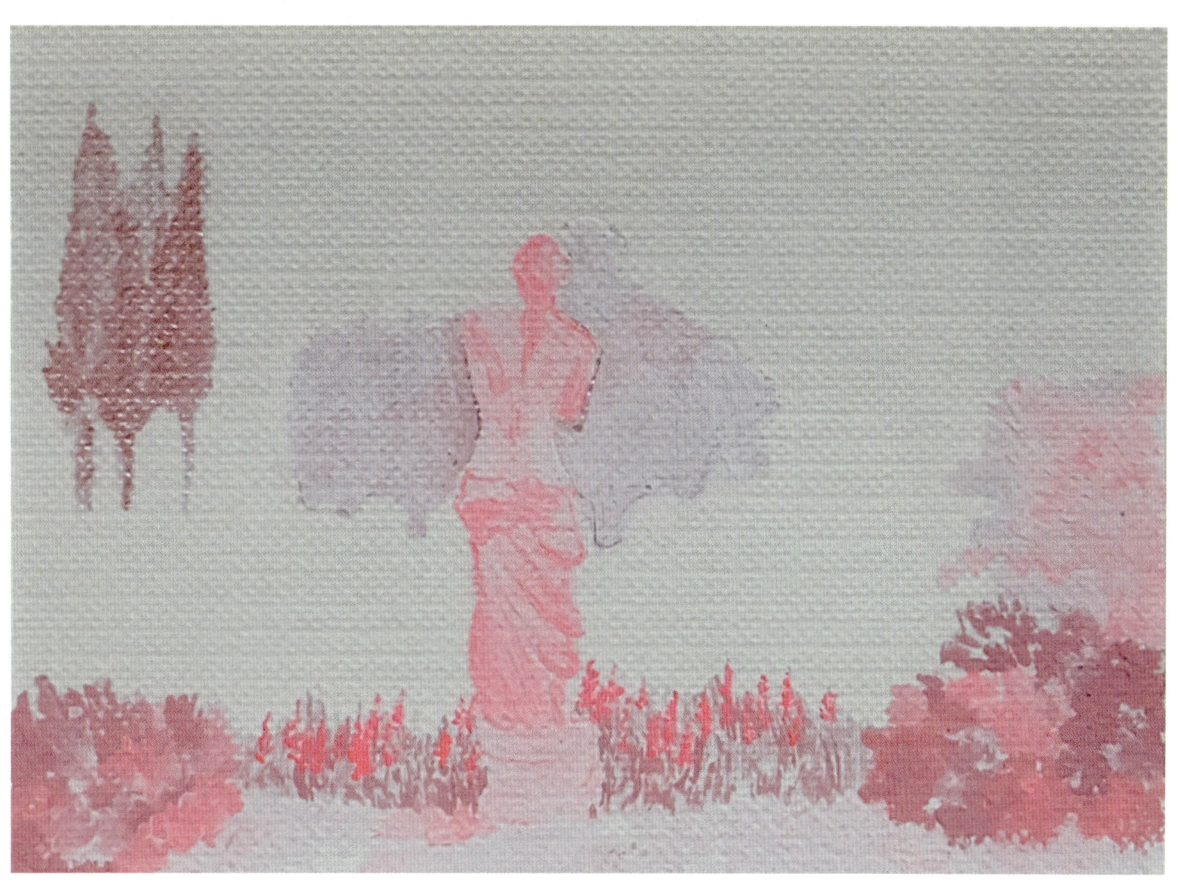

The Owner, 2015

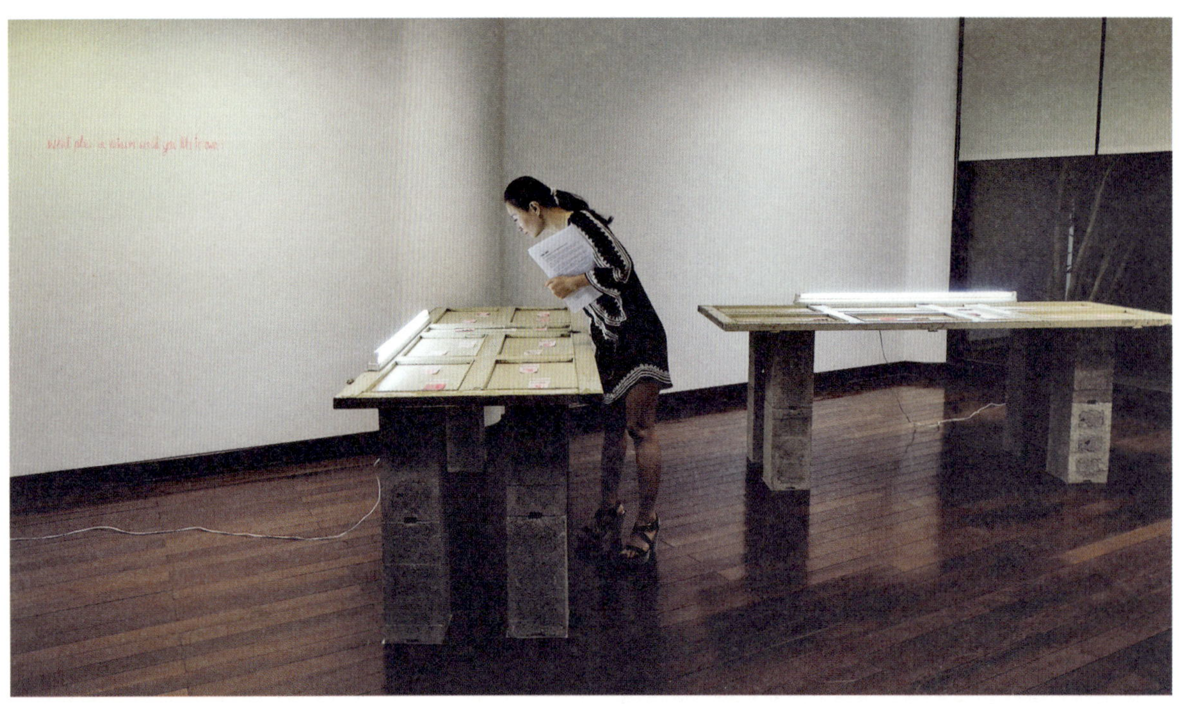

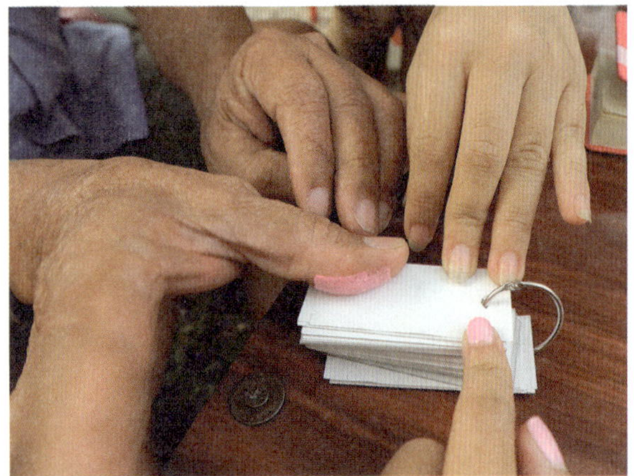

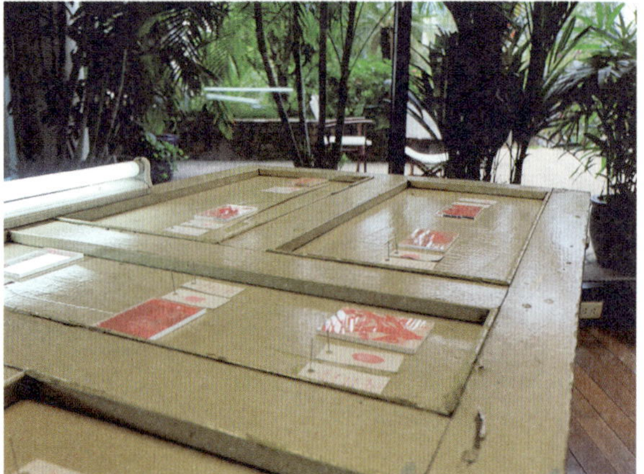

The Owner, 2015

way you produce alternative narratives and contents.
OA: In an exhibition, I show an original image as a drawing or painting, which can make people go through the history, the memory of a country. I just give them an image as a map, as a hint. Although I am not a historian or an anthropologist, I still need historians and anthropologists to come to work with me, and maybe to spread the word about my work to a wider audience. For me that would actually be a dream come true. Especially, because I have a different approach than they have: when I work in the public space, I approach people by asking whether they would like to spend time with me. That is very important. Every work of mine is about conversation. I never introduce myself as an artist or anthropologist. I just go as a human, as a friend who wants to share something. Once I go back to my studio, that conversation becomes an art piece, yes, but I still respect the people I have met ...

YM: ... and that leads to a huge difference between your practice in comparison to other anthropological approaches: you don't work with the stories you are being told in a sense that you don't make them a public part of your works. The only thing we, the audience, see are the drawings. We don't know the stories of those people. They remain an invisible space. How did this lead you to an interest in broader social and historical topics?

OA: This happened through a work titled *The Owner.* I did it in Vietnam, where I stayed at the Sàn Art Laboratory, Session 6 at Sàn Art, Ho Chi Minh City, for six months. I didn't have any real idea of Vietnam in my mind. So I thought six months are not enough time to know the whole country. I looked at the shape of Vietnam – it has this S form – and thought maybe people in these different parts can tell me their stories if I ask them one question: "What place would you like to own?" I travelled through Vietnam along the answers of these people. In that way I got to know the country. After the war people had moved everywhere. I thought that they still must have places of which they dream and that I have to go to these dream places. I talked to fifteen people of different ages in the South and to fifteen people in the North. Older people in the South would want to own a place in the North, which is connected to the post-war history.

It made the Vietnamese hopes and wishes visible and who they would like to be. It is not really scientific history or politics, but it is a way to find another existing history. The owners gave me their fingerprint. I used pink colour for that as well as for my drawings. The reason is that pink, for me, is not a real colour. It is a chemical colour. And the answer to my question could also not be real. In addition, there is this story of the goddess Ausa who would give life to the world by touching everything, trees, people etc. with her finger. This goddess is pink. But of course like the colour itself, she is not real.

YM: The fingerprint, however, is very real and also has a forensic feel about it. What was your idea behind that?

OA: The fingerprint is not only connected to that story but also to the fact that the people I talked to wanted to own that dream place. And if you really own anything at all, it is your identity. Especially the elderly people first got worried when I asked them for their fingerprint, because it reminded them of police activities. So they would be worried that I really wanted to move them somewhere. But once they realised that I was using pink colour for it, they understood that it was not real.

YM: Have they ever seen the finished work?

OA: Yes, I would either send it to them via e-mail or as for the older people I would show them the original. But then I had to tell them that I could not give them the original, as it was an artwork. I explained that the project was also about their dream being seen by an audience in the world. They are of course still the owners of their dream. But it is not only about imagination, it is also about beautiful images of real places so that people get inspired to visit the real place and through that learn about their histories. For me the real thing is as beautiful as the art piece in the gallery. You do not have to come to an exhibition only to listen to an artist but also to see things differently. That is my point and it is ongoing. I do not want to be an artist whose work just fits on the floor of an art space and say: "Look, this is my work". For me it goes much further than that. It is about learning, for the audience, but I am learning, too.

YM: In that sense your practice is very much about being a shared experience, not only the work itself but also the perception of it. It is about learning from each other. The people you talk to learn as much from you as you learn from them. Does this also apply to the work you are developing here in Berlin?

OA: Yes, absolutely.

YM: Maybe we could go one step back first: with your residency at Künstlerhaus Bethanien you came to Europe for the first time. What did that do for you?

OA: To be honest, the first day I did not feel a culture shock. For me it was more like: "Ah, ok, hello Berlin ..." A German friend of mine would drive me around and say: "Look, this is your Berlin." And I was like: "Yes ..., but it does not feel that different ..." Unter den Linden, for example, reminds me of Vietnam. For me Asia already has many European influences and vice versa I see Asian influences here. For example, there are Asian people from my generation who have lived here for a long time and go back now to open small business like small cafés or bars. So for me it was not a big "wow moment" on the first day.

YM: Many people would say that this residency in Berlin is a major step in your career as you made it into a "centre" of contemporary art. I mean especially from a European or US-American perspective many art professionals assume that a non-Euro-American artist can only make it if they get a platform in a "Western" context. I do not share this opinion as I think that there are many "centres" outside Euro-America that are just as relevant. The definition of what a "centre" is or could be is extremely subjective.

OA: For me it is really not important to make it as an artist in Europe or in the US, it has never been. I always wanted to work locally, to be a local artist who then reaches out to the world. Also, I don't think to be a local artist I have to constantly work on identity issues or have to try to be "authentic". I can be true to myself and to my context by producing work that still has the local connection but goes beyond these rather restraining ideas of identity etc. I did not come to Berlin to present myself as "the Thai artist", but as an artist.

YM: Yes, I agree that the focus should always be on the artist, their work and everything else comes with it – or doesn't. So how are you proceeding here in Berlin?

OA: While I'm in Berlin, I don't want to travel much but focus on people here. Compared to Vietnam, where I would go everywhere, it is more difficult here because of little things, for example the weather. Most of my time here has been during winter. In Asia, I could go out most of the time. Until now a big part of my work took place outside, not in a studio. So in Berlin I needed a lot of luck to meet people. In the beginning, I felt that I should just go with the flow and take my chances. I thought I would need to see the city more and to get to know it better. But of course there is a schedule, in the sense that my residency is time-limited, that there is an up-coming exhibition as part of it etc. I still try to be relaxed and natural as that is an important aspect of my practice.

At some point I missed my home and the food. So I went

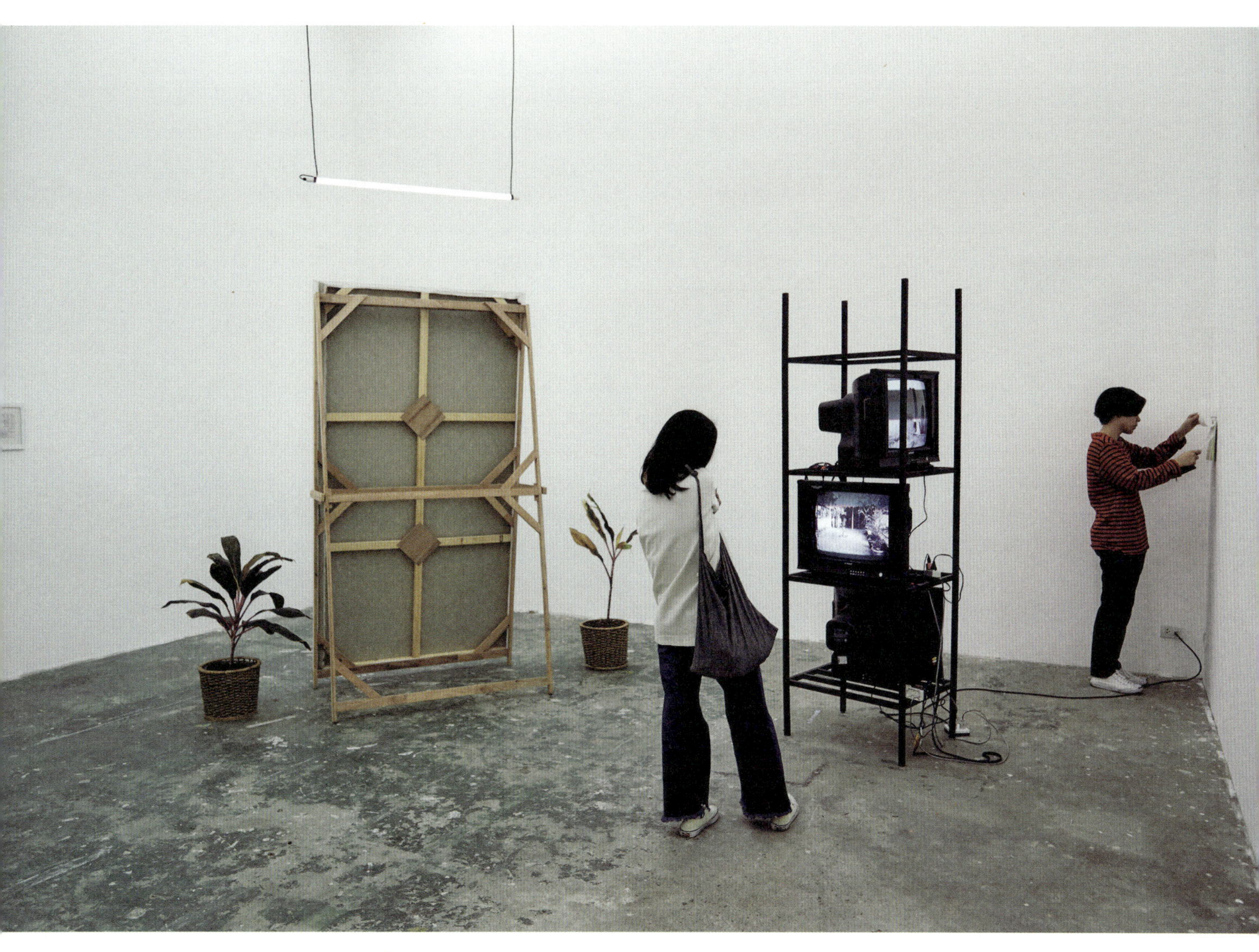

Zones and Verbs, 2016

to the "Thai Park" in Berlin. Suddenly, this woman sat next to me. We had a conversation in my language and after a while I knew I could ask her anything. And I asked her – I don't know why: "This is 'Thai Park', but why is there Vietnamese food?" And she said: "The Vietnamese food is made by my husband." I was really surprised because Thai people never have relationships with Vietnamese people. I would have rather expected her to have a German husband as many Thai people living in Europe have European partners. That made me very curious and I asked her whether we could meet again. The Berlin project basically started with this woman. She had two Vietnamese husbands, the first one was from South Vietnam, and the second one is from North Vietnam. Both of them, the woman and her husband, are German citizens. They speak German. So Berlin turned out to reflect this really interesting culmination of what I had seen and done before, because apart from being Berlin you also find a little bit of Thai, a little bit of Vietnam and a little bit of Cambodia.

YM: Where did this realisation take you?

OA: I also met a Thai man, who is a friend of a friend. He brought me to a Thai temple saying that if I wanted to eat free Thai food or if I needed some kind of feel of home I should go there. When I got back to the studio I was thinking about my luck to have met the lady in connection with my project in Vietnam. I also started to think about home and what makes it specific apart from what everybody knows about it, which is the food and Buddha ... Because of that and the small temple here in Berlin, I started to think more about spirituality at home. There is firstly the human being in our world, and secondly there is the soul or the spirit. In addition, I thought about the German context. So I am working on these three things. When I visited the temple again, a monk came up to me. He asked: "What do you think about my outfit?" I said that it didn't look like the outfits of monks in Thailand; of course it didn't because of winter. He had just used some fabric to wrap himself up in it. So we started to talk about how to live in this different context of Germany as a monk coming from far away, having to live in a small community. I also talked with the Thai lady about this question. How do you connect? As these conversations are so relevant, I decided that the Berlin project was going to have sound. It is the first time I will be using sound, which is going to be the voices of the people I met. I will pick sentences from these conversations. It is going to be a collage in Vietnamese, English, German and Thai. And it will seem as if they are talking to each other. But these "conversations" will actually be created by me. I will choose sentences that show how I perceived their relations.

YM: I understand that the conversations you had here were guided by the question of having to live in a foreign cultural context, in this case Germany. As much as this is interesting and important, I still wonder what else made these encounters so special for you?

OA: The conversations I had with the monk, for example, were conversations that I could not have had in Thailand. There I could not even talk to a monk and I definitively could not ask the questions I asked here. Or, rather, in Thailand you really would have to find the right monk. Here it is much more open. The same applies to the Thai woman. We had very different conversations from those we would have had if we had met in Thailand.

YM: You mentioned that you were initially thinking of spirituality in the sense of the human being, the soul and the spirit. Who else did you have conversations with to get deeper into this rather complex topic?

OA: I met a young man who splits his time between here and Asia. He can speak seven languages. Then I have a friend based in Germany who goes to Thailand frequently and speaks Thai very well. In the temple, I also met a German man who is a monk. And I met a Vietnamese nun. So this installation will be with and about people who live in the "human world" and those who live in the "spiritual world". Right now it is about ten people: one half working in the "spiritual world", the other half in the "human world". I met them all completely by chance.

YM: What about drawings, will they also be part of the work?

OA: Yes. I created drawings with forms that developed through the ten conversations. For me these forms will link to the sound in the room. I created them as a pattern, which will be printed on wallpaper mounted in the room where you will listen to the fragments I chose from the conversations. The forms have warm colours, earth tones, close to the skin colours of people. You will use your ears, your eyes and maybe get lost in the different languages and cultures. This is a good way to make you try to find out what it actually is. What is Thai, where is Vietnam, why Germany? This can make the audience try to see more than what they believe to know.

YM: This shows how the stay in Berlin has furthered your practice. It is very coherent, because it connects to the projects that you have done before, but at the same time it also adds new aspects in terms of content and form.

OA: Yes, that is true. I will also create a QR code. It will lead to a website where some of the sentences will be translated, but the website will be online only for about two weeks after the opening of the exhibition. In the exhibition itself, you will not understand everything. So you will also miss things. And I think that it is important to have these moments of missing links, of being lost in translation.

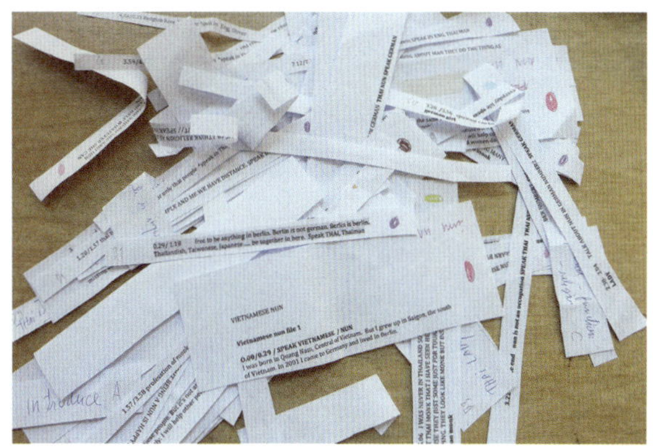

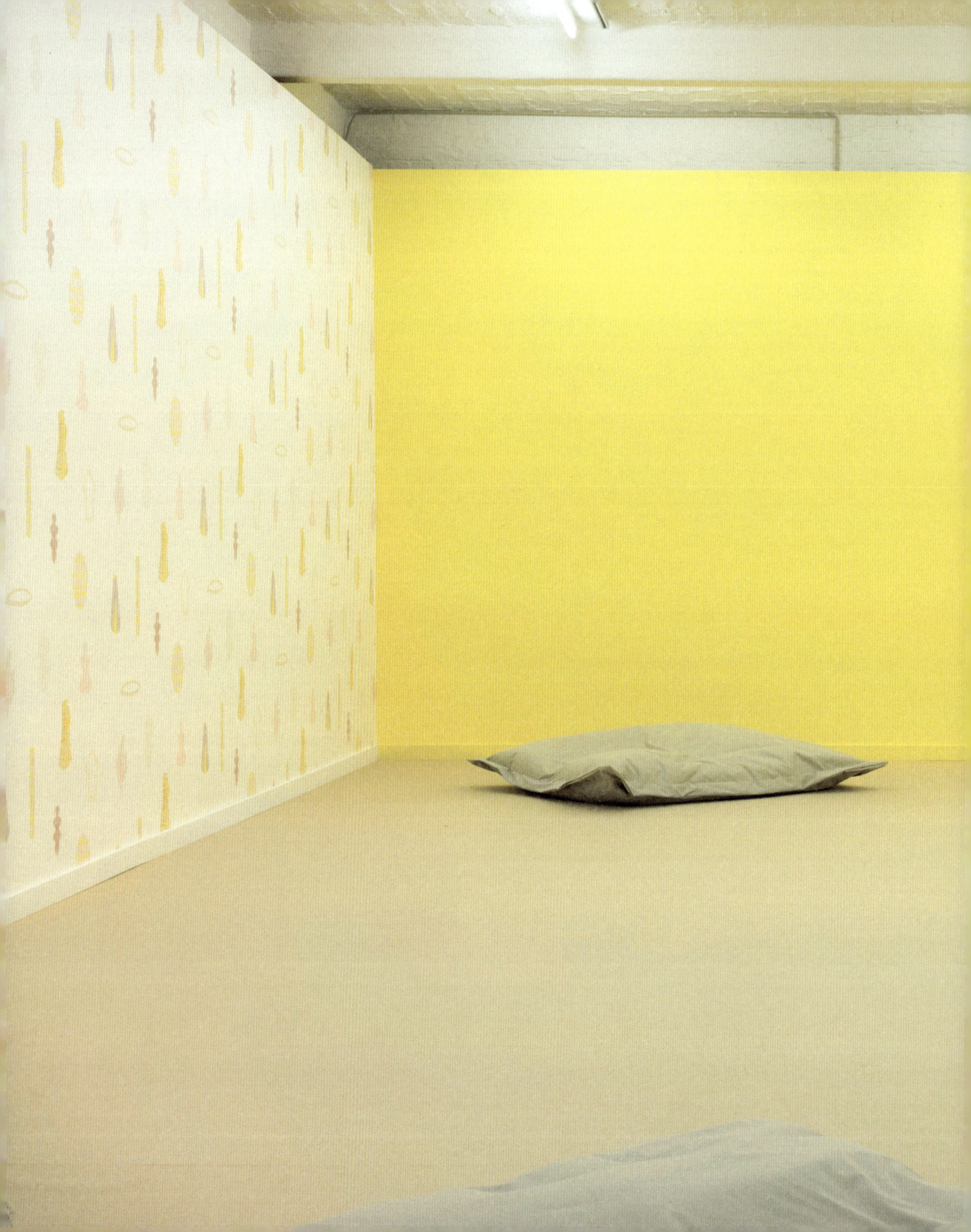

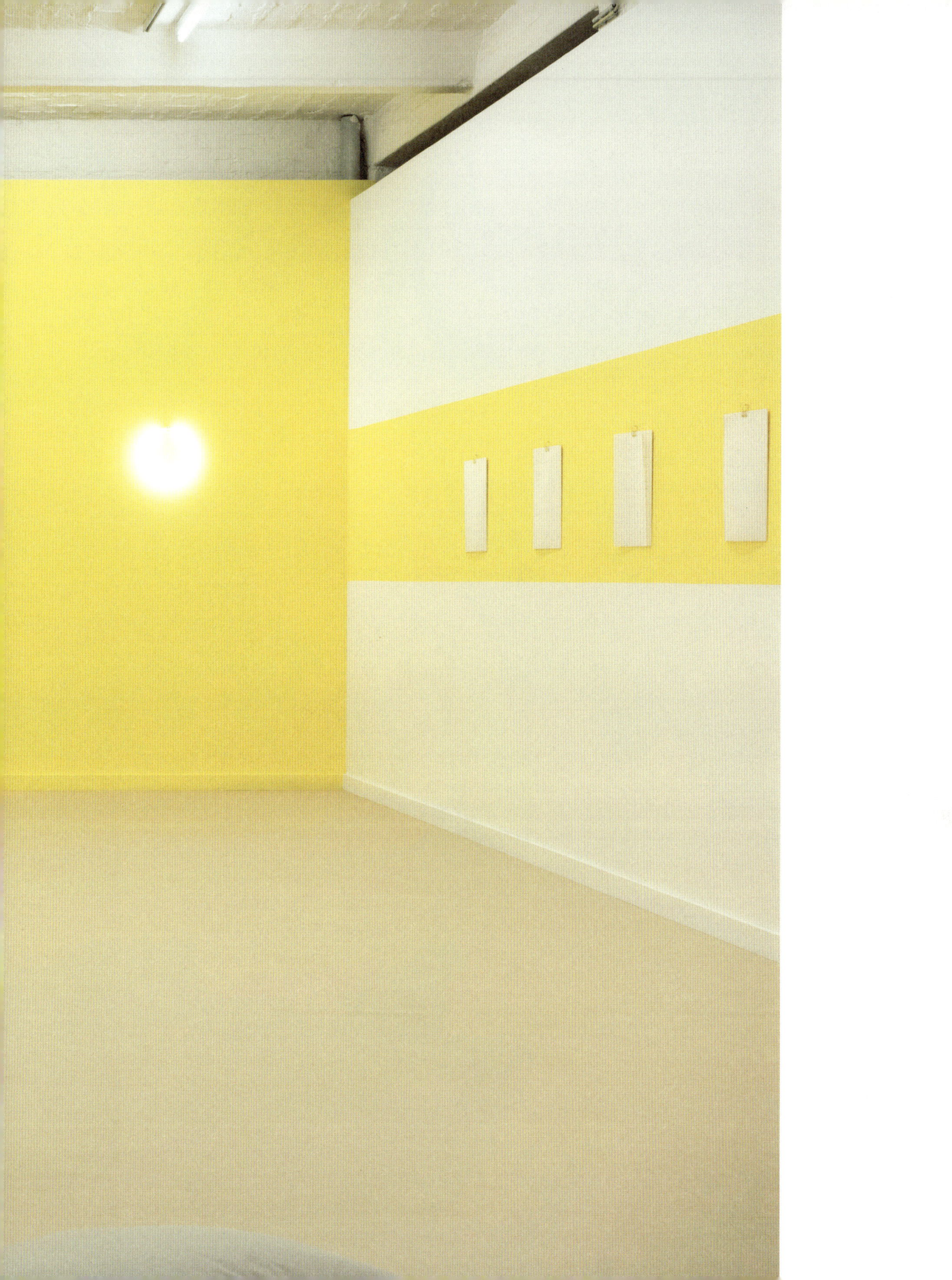

List of Works

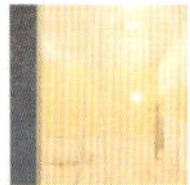

Exit – Entrance, 2017
Installation: wallpaper with printed drawings, 10 sheets of handwritten text, QR code, light, curtain, 2 floor cushions, sound (65 min., co-editor: Pedro Ferreira)
Künstlerhaus Bethanien, Berlin

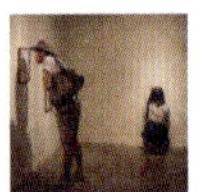

What Are They Doing Inside?, 2013
Installation: 29 drawings (pigment ink 0.03), different sizes
Speedy Grandma, Bangkok

What Are They Doing Inside?, 2013 (detail)
Asakusa, Tokyo
Pen on paper (pigment ink 0.03), size of paper: 27 x 35.5 cm, size of drawing: 4.7 x 6.5 cm

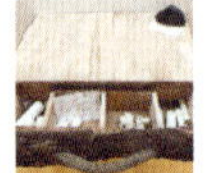

Follow Me, 2013
Installation: drawer, notebook, light, stone, pieces of paper (drawing, text, e-mail)
Bangkok Art and Culture Centre

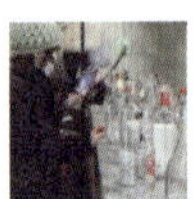
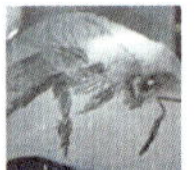

Breathing Bubbles, 2013
Installation: glass bottles with drawings, partly filled with water, ledge of concrete
Kanagawa Arts Theatre, Yokohama

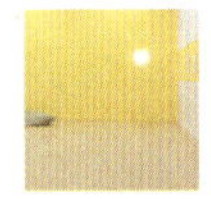
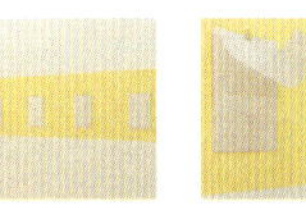

Exit – Entrance, 2017

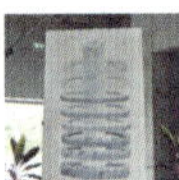

Meditating Painting, 2016
Installation: painting (oil on linen) on wooden easel, 2 plants (drymoda siamenses), pillow, 2 stools, mat.
Performance: The process of making *Meditating Painting* in a period of 30 days in June 2016, morning routine/praying starting at 7.30am, evening routine/praying starting at 5.30pm
The Buddhadasa Indapanno Archives, Wachirabenchathat Park (aka Rodfai Park or State Railway Public Park), Bangkok

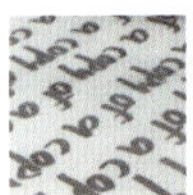
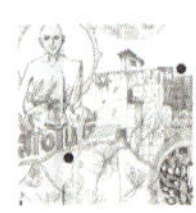

Drifting Map of Bangkok, 2012
Broadsheet
Bangkok Art and Culture Centre

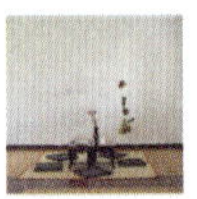

Come In, 2014
Installation: table, 2 mats, 5 cushions, vase with lotus flowers, fruits, notebook with drawings, photo album with drawings, drawings on the wall
Sa Sa Art Projects, Phnom Penh

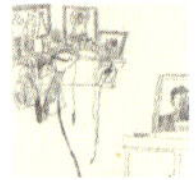
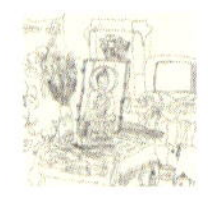

Come In, 2014 (details)
Series of 15 drawings in postcard format, displayed in photo album, size: 20 x 23 cm

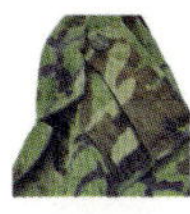

My Godfather, 2014–15
Military jacket with hand-sewn gold thread

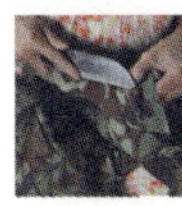

My Godfather: She Preserves Godfather's Dignity, 2014–15
Single-channel video with sound, 4:22 min.
The artist's godmother is cutting the label of the godfather's name.

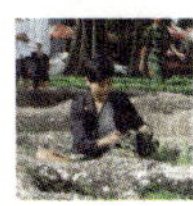 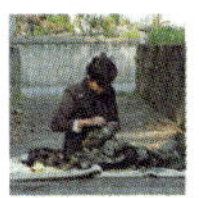 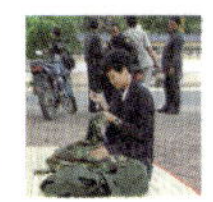

My Godfather: War Journey, 2014–15
3 videos of the artist sewing the gold thread in the jacket. The performance was done in public space in Ho Chi Minh City (co-editor: Ta Minh Duc). Okinawa (co-editor: Koji Monotake) and Phnom Penh (co-editor: Dara Kong).

The Owner, 2015
Acrylic on canvas paper, 6.5 x 9 cm

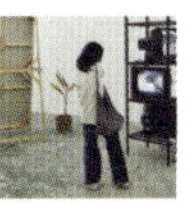

Zones and Verbs, 2016
Installation: painting, video, photos, drawings, texts
Cartel, Bangkok

Biography

Orawan Arunrak
Born 1985 in Bangkok, Thailand,
where she lives and works

EDUCATION

2007 BFA (Printmaking), Department of Fine Arts, King Mongkut's Institute of Technology Ladkrabang, Bangkok

RESIDENCIES

2016–17 Artist-in-residence programme of KfW Stiftung at Künstlerhaus Bethanien, Berlin

2014–15 Sàn Art Laboratory, Session 6, Sàn Art, Ho Chi Minh City

2014 Pisaot Experimental Arts Residency, Sa Sa Art Projects, Phnom Penh

SELECTED SOLO EXHIBITIONS

2016 *Zones and Verbs*, Cartel, Bangkok

2014 *Dear Duang Daao*, Duang Daao Cafe, Ikebukuro, Japan

2013 *What Are They Doing Inside?*, Speedy Grandma, Bangkok

2008 *Brandnew: Supernoyz*, Tadu Contemporary Art, Bangkok

SELECTED GROUP EXHIBITIONS

2017 *Star*, Rocky Shore Inaugural Exhibition, Tokyo

2016 *Public Spirits*, Centre for Contemporary Art Ujazdowski Castle, Warsaw

2015 *Choose to Move*, Sàn Art, Ho Chi Minh City

2014–15 *Rates of Exchange, Un-Compared: Contemporary Art in Bangkok and Phnom Penh*, H Gallery, Bangkok, SA SA BASSAC, Phnom Penh

2014 *Experimental Video Art Exhibition*, Thai-European Friendship 2004–2014 (EVA project), Bangkok Art and Culture Centre, Bangkok

2013 *Resort*, Bangkok Art and Culture Centre, Bangkok The Performing Arts Meeting, Kanagawa Arts Theatre (KATT), Yokohama

2012 *Messy Sky, Les Fleurs Americaines*, Frac Île-de-France, Le Plateau, Paris
Drifting Map, BACC Experimental: Temporary Storage #01, Bangkok Art and Culture Centre, Bangkok

2011 *Warning*, National School Beaux-Arts, Paris
City of Angels/Identity Crisis, Galerie 59 Rivoli, Paris

2007 *Experimental Video Exhibition*, Thai-European Friendship, The Queen Sirikit National Convertion Center, Bangkok, Silpakorn University, Nakhon Pathom, Bundipatanasilpa Institute, Ladkabang, Burapa University, Chiang Mai University, and King Mungkut's Institute of Teshnology Ladkabang, Thailand

About the authors:

Roger Nelson is an art historian and independent curator based in Phnom Penh, and recently submitted his PhD at the University of Melbourne, addressing modernity and contemporaneity in "Cambodian arts" after independence. His writing has been published in scholarly journals, specialist art magazines, books and exhibition catalogues internationally. He has curated exhibitions and other projects in Australia, Cambodia, Singapore, Thailand and Vietnam, including most recently, *People, Money, Ghosts (Movement as Metaphor)* at Bangkok's Jim Thompson Art Center (2017). In 2015–16 Nelson participated in the Getty Foundation's research program, *Ambitious Alignments: New Histories of Southeast Asian Art*, and his essay on the Cambodian painter Nhek Dim (1934–78) will appear in a forthcoming volume of the same title. He has spoken at conferences internationally, including at New York's Museum of Modern Art and at the National Gallery Singapore. Nelson is a co-founding co-editor of the new scholarly journal, *SOUTHEAST OF NOW: Directions in Contemporary and Modern Art in Asia*, published in print and online by the National University of Singapore Press.

Yvette Mutumba is co-founder and editor-in-chief of the art magazine *Contemporary And* (C&). She is part of the curatorial team of the 10th Berlin Biennial (June, 9th to September 9th 2018). From 2012 to 2016 she was curator at Weltkulturen Museum, Frankfurt. Here she co-curated the major exhibitions *Foreign Exchange – or the stories you wouldn't tell a stranger*, *El Hadji Sy: Paintings, Performance, Politics* and *A Labour of Love*. In 2016 she co-curated *Focus: African Perspectives* of The Armory Show, New York. Mutumba studied Art History at Freie Universität, Berlin and holds a PhD from Birkbeck, University of London. As author and editor she has published numerous texts/books on contemporary art from African perspectives as well as Global Art History. Most recent publication: *I am built inside you*, ed. by ifa and *C&* (Sternberg Press, April 2017).

Orawan Arunrak
Exit – Entrance
With an essay by Roger Nelson and an interview by Yvette Mutumba

Editors Herausgeber
Nicola Müllerschön
Christoph Tannert

Künstlerhaus Bethanien GmbH
Kohlfurter Str. 41/43
Showroom/Schauraum:
Kottbusser Str. 10
D-10999 Berlin
www.bethanien.de

Artistic Director
Künstlerische Leitung
Christoph Tannert

Administrative Director
Kaufmännische Leitung
Andrea Boche

International Studio Programme
Internationales Atelierprogramm
Valeria Schulte-Fischedick

Press & PR Presse
Christina Sickert

Administration Verwaltung
Ute Werner

Technical Staff Technik
Toni Lebkücher, Peter Rosemann

KfW Stiftung
Palmengartenstraße 5–9
D-60325 Frankfurt am Main
www.kfw-stiftung.de

Executive Director
Geschäftsführer
Bernd Siegfried

Programme Manager
Arts and Culture
Programmleiterin Kunst und Kultur
Nicola Müllerschön

Editing Redaktion
Christoph Tannert
Valeria Schulte-Fischedick
Malina Lauterbach

Copy-editing and Translation
Lektorat und Übersetzung
Aymone Rassaerts

Project Management/Design
Thorsten Probst/angenehme-gestaltung

Photos
Orawan Arunrak 6, 19, 25, 41–43, 52, 57
Wolfgang Bellwinkel 6, 7, 20–24, 28, 29, 32–38, 58, 59 / Pol Dussaussois Martinez 11, 12 / Sittidech Nuhuang 14, 15 Surat Setsaeng 55 / Lim Sokchanlina 44, 46, 47

Production Gesamtherstellung
Druckerei Kettler, Bönen

Published by Erschienen im
Verlag Kettler, Dortmund
www.verlag-kettler.de

This catalogue is published on the occasion of the exhibition *Exit – Entrance* by Orawan Arunrak, International Studio Programme, Künstlerhaus Bethanien, Berlin, May 25 to June 18, 2017. Orawan Arunrak is a grantee of KfW Stiftung, Frankfurt am Main.

Der Katalog erscheint anlässlich der Ausstellung *Exit – Entrance* von Orawan Arunrak im Rahmen des Internationalen Atelierprogramms des Künstlerhauses Bethanien, Berlin, vom 25. Mai bis 18. Juni 2017. Orawan Arunrak ist Stipendiatin der KfW Stiftung, Frankfurt am Main.

The artist would like to acknowledge:
Family and friends in Thailand, Cambodia, Vietnam and Japan, Künstlerhaus Bethanien staff, Nicola Müllerschön, Roger Nelson, Pedro Ferreira, Jirapat and Napat Vatanakuljaras, Wolfgang Bellwinkel, Sorayut Aiemueayut, Đỗ Tường Linh, Leanh Pham, Nut Srisu-wan, Thitipol Panyalimpanun, Pojai Akratanakul, Marie-Hélène Gutberlet, Yvette Mutumba, Kanako Hayashi, Lyuyen Uyenly, P'Prim family, monk and nun in Thai temple in Berlin, Vietnamese nun at Chua Linh Thứu/Berlin, Oliver Raendchen, Tom Meddings, Supapong Laodheerasiri, Natnaran Bualoy, Knakorn Kachacheewa, Arin Rungjang, Pichaya Suphavanij, Chitti Kasemkitvatana, Mit Jai Inn, Marie Elaine, Poomin Wongsing

KÜNSTLERHAUS BETHANIEN

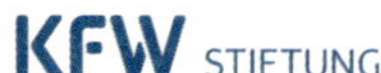

ISBN 978-3-86206-671-1

ORAWAN ARUNRAK

EXIT – ENTRANCE

KÜNSTLERHAUS BETHANIEN

KFW STIFTUNG

Preface

Promoting cultural diversity is one of the primary goals of the foundation KfW Stiftung. Together with the cultural centre Künstlerhaus Bethanien, we have set up an artist-in-residence programme that seeks to stimulate intercultural dialogue by providing artists from Latin America, Africa and Asia with the opportunity to spend twelve months in Berlin. Besides encouraging artistic production and critical reflection, the programme facilitates encounters between those working in arts and culture. The infrastructure and the international environment of the cultural centre offer a suitable setting, allowing participants to try out new ideas, to engage in debates and to carry out projects.

Artists are often expected to show site-specific authenticity devoid of local colour and equally to produce universally intelligible works outside the global mainstream. Given this situation, how do artists' origins impact the perception of their works of art? Our artist-in-residence programme does not present artists as representatives of a particular country. Rather, it highlights the existing links between international networks on the one hand and the examination of specific geographic and culturally defined places on the other, thus generating novel ways of thinking and perceiving.

Die Stärkung kultureller Vielfalt ist ein besonderes Anliegen der KfW Stiftung. Mit dem Ziel, den interkulturellen Dialog voranzutreiben, realisieren wir in Kooperation mit dem Künstlerhaus Bethanien ein Atelierprogramm, das Künstlern aus Lateinamerika, Afrika und Asien einen zwölfmonatigen Aufenthalt in Berlin ermöglicht. Künstlerische Produktion und kritische Reflexion sollen ebenso gefördert werden wie der Austausch mit anderen Kunst- und Kulturschaffenden. Die Infrastruktur und das internationale Umfeld des Künstlerhauses bieten eine Plattform zu experimentieren, zu diskutieren und Projekte zu realisieren.

Welche Rolle spielt jedoch die Herkunft eines Künstlers für die Rezeption seines Werks, wenn einerseits ortsspezifische Authentizität ohne Lokalkolorit, andererseits universelle Lesbarkeit ohne globalen Mainstream erwartet wird? Unser Atelierprogramm teilt Künstlern nicht die Rolle von nationalen Repräsentanten zu. Vielmehr zeigt sich, dass internationale Vernetzung und die Auseinandersetzung mit bestimmten geografischen und kulturell geprägten Orten miteinander verknüpft sind und so neue Denk- und Sichtweisen entstehen.

Ulrich Schröder
Board KfW Stiftung

Contents

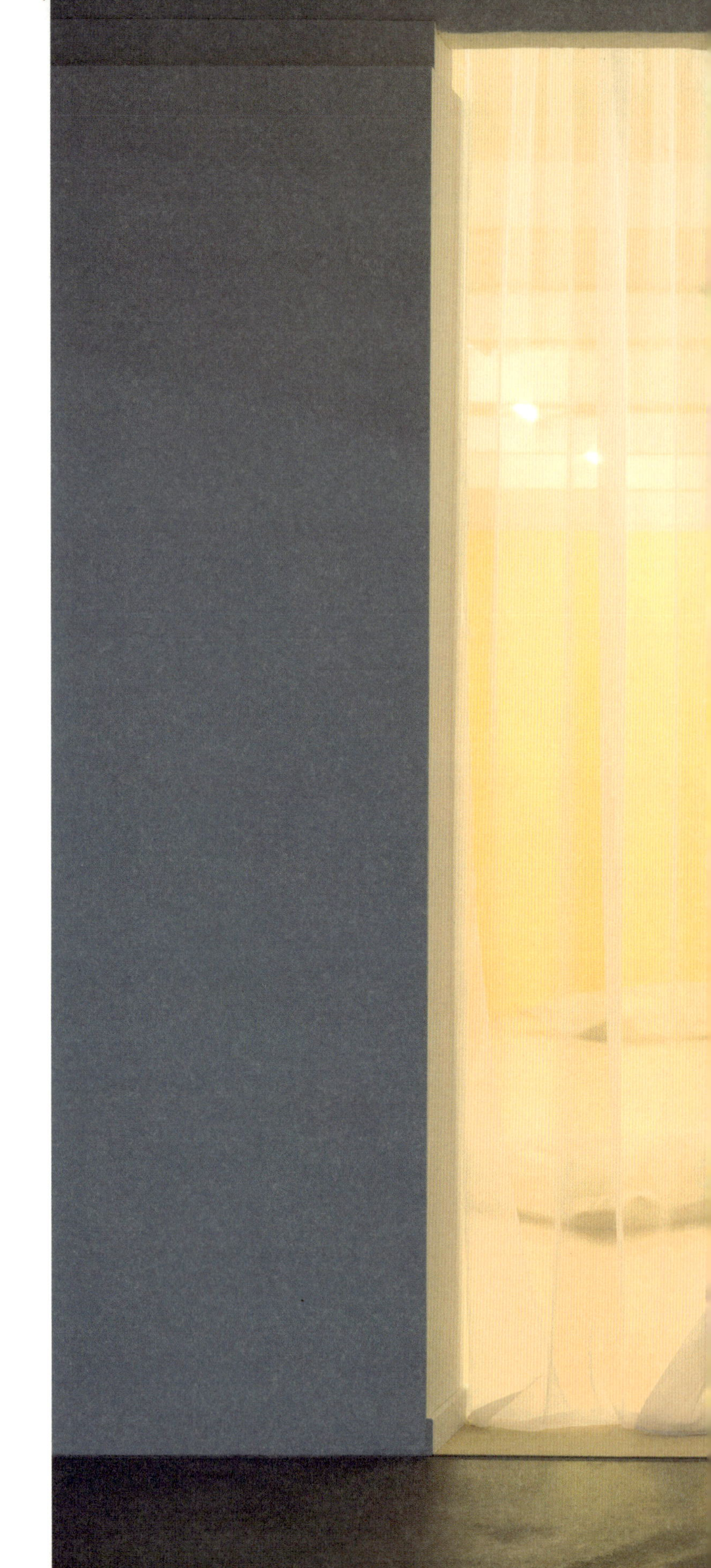

Exit – Entrance, 2017